How Social Networking Doubled My Business

By

Natalie Heeley

With Linda Dunscombe

First published in the United Kingdom in 2015 by Dreams Publishing

Copyright © Natalie Heeley 2015
www.natalieheeley.co.uk

Co-written by Linda Dunscombe
www.linda-dunscombe.co.uk

Illustrations © Claire Jenkins 2015
www.successanimated.co.uk

Photography © Sander Jurkiewicz
www.sanderjurkiewicz.com

A CIP catalogue record for this book is available from the British Library
Print Book: ISBN 978-0-9931467-0-1

Typeset by Shore Books, Blackborough End, King's Lynn, Norfolk
Printed and bound in Great Britain by Lightning Source

Contents

Foreword
by
Gemma Easdon and Beth Turner

"You are what you share" is what we believe to be true about the power of social media in today's world and we tested this the day we met Natalie Heeley for the first time.

Our curiosity began after being introduced to the product in the Autumn of 2013. The quality was clear and having spent 15 years as senior leaders in the John Lewis Partnership we instinctively knew that a great product like this, shared in the right way, was a recipe for business success.

Our research naturally started with social media, where Natalie's world-leading business growth quickly became apparent. The culture we upheld in John Lewis means that we do not just value business success on outcomes alone as these are only part of the story; the core of success is in the behaviour and attitude of how it is achieved.

On social media we didn't just see a world-leading Distributor who topped the tables, we also saw a 37-year-old single mum of two young children who portrayed courage, honesty and integrity in business. THAT was why we got in touch with Natalie and choose her as our sponsor.

All that remained in putting social media to the test was when we met Natalie for the first time in January 2014 when we found that she is indeed exactly what she chooses to share on social media.

Gemma Easdon and Beth Turner

I dedicate this book…

To my Mum, Jan Whittaker, for having the courage to embrace Network Marketing 18 years ago and of course to Will and Rosie who have always been my reason and never my excuse.

How Social Networking
Doubled My Business

Chapter One

Mother Usually Knows Best!

We all have dreams, desires and ambitions. Sometimes, luck gives us a helping hand and we find that through hard work and application some of those dreams come true.

I am one of the top Network Distributors in the UK today. I have built a business that delivers everything I want in terms of lifestyle, income and future financial security. I'm not sure that luck has played a very big role in my success, but hard work and application certainly have.

I don't have all the answers, nor do I have a magic wand or a fairy godmother to smooth the way. What I do have to offer you is my story. You will see that I am not superwoman. I am not extraordinary. Everything I have done can be replicated. I am a normal woman - daughter, sister, mother, partner, and friend.

If I can do it then so can you.

Sometimes, it's all about timing. I'd had so many chances to become part of a success-ful Network Marketing business, but I simply didn't want to know. My mother already had a very well established Network. To me, pretty much any job seemed preferable to following my Mum into her business. I suppose back then I didn't really understand what she did and I certainly had no idea how well she did at it. I had watched her build a very respectable team, so I knew something of what it was all about. But I had no interest and refused to listen to anything positive she had to say about it. Mum would have loved me to join her much earlier than I finally did, she couldn't understand my reluctance. She was offering me a proven opportunity to build myself a business and earn a good income. As far as I was concerned, it wasn't right for me, not back then and not for a variety of reasons. I suppose looking back my refusal to even consider it as an option was all tied up with the fact that it was my mother and I was still young enough to believe that I knew better. Maybe it was a touch of lingering teenage rebellion. Also, the business seemed in the early days to be geared towards middle-aged people. Network Marketing certainly wasn't cool, interesting or sexy, at least not to my young eyes.

Mum first began her journey after my parents' split up. She was used to being busy, running a large home and looking after her husband

and three children. She needed an income and felt that she had few skills to take into the job marketplace. She found her way into Network Marketing almost by accident, as these things so often are. It wasn't a route she had ever considered and I understand she was quite reluctant to begin with. But she soon found her marketing feet and although domestic life had drained away some of her confidence she had always been a very social person and that helped her to move forward.

I was sixteen when my Mum and Dad divorced. It was incredibly difficult for me. I suppose I was aware that Mum wasn't happy, but it had never occurred to me that my secure family unit could be torn apart. As a teenager I had no desire to move away from the house I had grown up in so I stayed with my Dad. My brother was away at University and my little seven-year-old sister left to go and live with Mum.

It wasn't easy. My father couldn't cook and he struggled to look after the house. He was unhappy and I blamed my mother for break-ing us all up. Everything had changed and none of it for the better. I couldn't understand why she had ruined everything. The fact that she started her Network Marketing business at around the same time probably added to my resistance to it. Plus, whenever I went to see her the phone would be ringing, constantly demanding her attention and taking her away from me. In those days the telephone and face to face were the only way to build a business. No Social Media back in 1992! I can see now that back then I resented the business and all my associated memories around it were negative.

If anyone had asked me then what I wanted to do with my life, any form of Direct Selling or Network Marketing would have been at the very bottom of any list. The expression 'never in a million years' comes to mind.

**But never is a long time
and everything changes.**

I had a pretty idyllic childhood up until the time of my parents' divorce. A nice house, great holidays, security and a Mum at home who kept everything running smoothly. My Dad worked long hours and upheld a strong work ethic. I started babysitting when I was twelve and we were all encouraged to make our own money. We never went without, although we quickly learnt that Dad was always more generous at topping up incomes and rewarding enterprise.

It was a good lesson and one that stayed with me.

It was my father who encouraged me to travel and I went backpacking across the world. I took a gap year after finishing my A levels and then itchy feet carried me off again as soon as I finished University. I worked for a charity in Africa to build a nursery school in the Massai Mara reserve and spent the rest of my time travelling on the cheap. It made me strong and resilient and gave me the belief that life is an adventure and anything is possible. A message that at times, in darker days, I lost sight of.

My Dad came and joined me for part of the trip and decided that, at sixty, he wasn't too old for a bit of backpacking himself. So off he went trekking around the world until finally setting himself down for several years in South Africa.

After a six-month stint of travelling through Australia, America and Fiji, I finally returned home and knew it was time for me to find a job.

'Come and work with me,' my Mum said, trying once again to lure me into the business, 'you'll be so good at it and you could be earning great money in no time.'

I'd rather spend my days hopping on burning coals; I thought, but managed not to say. It never even occurred to me that she might be right. I simply had zero interest. And I wasn't the only one. My siblings had banned any talk about the business from the dinner table. Looking back, I can sympathise with my mother. All she wanted was what was best for us. We were too stubborn and we didn't see it that way at all. We just thought she was nagging, or maybe even desperate. It never occurred to me that she was offering me a great opportunity.

I'd rather spend my days hopping on burning coals, I thought

'I'll get you a job,' Chris, a family friend said to me one evening in the local village pub.

'Doing what?' I was a bit wary as he was always into some crazy scheme or another. If he answered 'selling buffalo milk' I wouldn't have been at all surprised.

'Selling advertising space for a local publication,' he replied, leaving me feeling a bit disappointed by its tameness.

But I needed a job and although not as exotic as selling buffalo milk, it was probably easier!

I was only twenty-two and in my first job I had a company car and was earning £16,000 plus bonuses, which was a lot of money back then. It was only a small company and Chris taught me the skills of being an entrepreneur as he was so passionate about his new venture.
It paid the bills and made me settle down for a while. I probably benefited from having the discipline of a proper job and set working hours after all my travelling. But sadly the economy and the business were struggling and ended up closing down. I went to work for a marketing agency as an account manager.

Of course, you can't keep a good man down and it wasn't too long before the ever-enterprising Chris was back in touch.

'Fuzzy brushes?' I repeated, totally confused by the conversation we were having.

'It's like chewing gum.' He told me on the telephone. 'Only it's a toothbrush. Come on, Nat, I really need your help.'

There was something irresistible about Chris. He had a passion and energy that made him hard to say no too. So, a short while later, I found myself driving around the country placing disposable chewable toothbrushes into the toilets at service stations, bars and airports. I enjoyed being out and about; it certainly seemed to suit me more than office work. The business seemed to do quite well and although I didn't see it as a career, I was happy enough with the job.

Chris was a very influential person in my life, although I'm not sure I fully realised it at the time. He taught me that hard work could make anything happen and, if you had an idea and the conviction to see it through then you owed it to yourself to try.

The trouble with Chris was that he was always moving on to the next big idea and apparently the logical next step from fuzzy brushes was to set up a speed-dating agency.

'It's all the rage in America,' he informed me confidently, now apparently a self-proclaimed expert after reading one article. 'You know whatever takes off over there soon crosses the pond.'

That irresistible passion and conviction worked again and somehow he managed to convince me. Together we set up a company that organised the dating events. He did all the IT stuff and funded the business, while I did the organising and all the legwork. I loved the thrill that came from setting up a new business and I was able to use my PR skills to get us some local news coverage. We set up in several different towns offering weekly sessions, but I was too shy and too self-conscious to host them myself. I stayed in the background and let my boyfriend of the time be the face of the business.

Amazingly, it was a really big success. Chris had called it right and the craze did cross the Atlantic. For a time it seemed as though the only way to find your next partner was via a speed-dating session. It was fun and challenging. We worked long hours and built the business up until one day a big London agency made us an offer we couldn't refuse and bought us out.

It was 2004 and by then I was happy to sell. I was expecting my first child and the business wasn't exactly great for pregnancy or motherhood. The hours were long and the pub/club environment was not going to work once my baby was born. The agency asked me to stay on to make sure the transition went smoothly so I worked as an employee, just briefly, until they made me redundant before my son, Will, was born.

I then took my first step into the world of Direct Selling by setting up a wooden toy business with my sister. We lugged heavy boxes to craft fairs and to people's houses to sell at parties. It was hard work and storing all the stock was a nightmare.

'I can offer a much easier way to earn some money,' Mum said, when I complained about the stacks of boxes everywhere I turned.

My sister Sam and I both groaned. Sam was just as anti about Network Marketing as I was.

Poor Mum sighed, shrugged her shoulders and left us to it. It must have been so infuriating and frustrating for her to see us struggle on, working hard and earning a pittance. Not surprisingly, the business didn't last for very long. It was a logistical nightmare. It did show me though the potential benefits of Direct Selling. Party plan was a powerful outlet for moving product and if the experience taught me nothing else, I did at least come away with a better understanding of how the Direct Selling process worked.

Motherhood naturally changed me and my priorities altered. I wanted to settle and security was now top of my desire list. I married Will's father in March 2005 at a beautiful ceremony in Cape Town, we said our vows looking out across the Indian Ocean. I wore a white dress with pretty red roses on it and it was a very happy period for me. I love Cape Town. My brother, his wife, Collette and their son Joshua, and my father were living out there at the time. I think I could have happily settled down alongside them in the shadow of Table Mountain. But our lives were back in England, as was my Mum and younger sister. So we said our goodbyes and headed home.

Our second child was born nine months later, a honeymoon baby who we called Rosie.

My husband was a teacher and I was at home with our two small children. Money was tight, but I knew I didn't want to go back out to work. Mum had always been at home for me, and my siblings, and I wanted the same secure, idyllic childhood for my babies as I had enjoyed. The reality though was that bills needed paying and living on one wage was not easy. It still never occurred to me that following my mother into her Network was the obvious step for me. If I thought about it at all (which I probably didn't) my view would be that I had no time to be running around to people's houses or spending hours on countless phone calls.

Mum had a totally different take on the situation and one day in May 2006 when Will was two and Rosie just five months old, she persuaded me to meet one of her friends Jayne Leach, at a Motorway service station. Not exactly a glamorous setting for an event that was about to change my life! I didn't know it at the time, but the lady who sat down and told me all about this amazing business that I could run from home and work around my children, was actually the Number One distributor in the country. Nor did I know what an important role she was going to play in my life. I must admit that hearing it all from another person made it sound interesting, tempting and totally different to what I thought my mother actually did. I found myself agreeing to do it there and then - why wouldn't I? It sounded fantastic and besides, Mum was buying my starter pack.

Back at home I put the kettle on while Mum cuddled Rosie and tickled Will. I made the coffee and when I turned round carrying two mugs I saw the sign-up papers and a pen on the table. I looked at her and she looked back at me. The time had finally come. I put the mugs down, picked up the pen and signed myself into the world of Network Marketing.

It's not your job to convince people

People will get involved when the time is right for them

The time had finally come – I signed myself into the world of Network Marketing.

How to begin building a network

Step One – Don't lose momentum
It is important to book a planning meeting with your sponsor as soon as possible. Preferably within forty-eight hours of joining a network.

Step Two – Knowledge before excitement
I know you want to rush out and tell everyone about the exciting journey you have signed up for. But I really do urge you to sit on it until you have had that first planning meeting.

**A little information can
be a dangerous thing!**

The temptation is to offload all the information that you have onto your friends and family. But you are in danger of alienating them with information overload, confusing them with half-remembered business plans and baffling them with dreams and ambitions.

Your sponsor will show you how to invite people to look at your product or service along with the business opportunity.

One of the things that have made my Network expand so wide and so fast is the availability of basic trainings that my group have put together. Thanks to Social Media they are easily accessible online via Facebook and unlisted YouTube videos. We send all newcomers to these resources as soon as they register.

Ask your sponsor to direct you to whatever online learning tools are available to you. Then spend the time to watch and listen and absorb as much information as you can before taking on the world.

Step Three – know why you want to do it

Work out what you want to achieve from this new adventure. Set some goals; build a Dream Book (see Chapter Three – How to build a Dream Book)

We all need to have a reason for our actions otherwise it is a struggle to maintain motivation.

Step Four – Be realistic

No Direct Selling or Network Marketing operation is a get-rich quick scheme. You need to be realistic and understand that you will only be successful if you commit to it as a realistic business opportunity.

That doesn't mean you can't run it alongside your existing work and lifestyle. You can build a Network as a part-time business and use it as an income top-up. But whether you want this to be a full-time career choice or a supplementary income, you still have to work at it.

A traditional start up business would require a financial investment of possibly several thousand pounds. You would then expect to work long hours for little reward while you got the business off the ground.

Network Marketing allows you to build a business for a tiny financial outlay. You can run it at your own pace and to suit your own circumstances. If you work hard for twelve months, you could be enjoying a good income. Five years hard work could set you up for life. But it won't happen without you driving it.

You are the accelerator and the anchor.

It really is up to you to decide what you want and how much time and effort you are willing to put into achieving it.

Step Five – Spread the word
With help and encouragement from your spon-

sor you should sit down and write a contact list. Don't delay; begin to do this as soon as you have signed up. Don't contact anyone before you have completed the planning and training sessions, but build the list as soon as you can.

Print out all contacts from Social Media including Facebook. If you have international contacts and want to go Global with your business, compile a UK list and a separate world-wide one.

Step Six – Be Positive and Proactive

Negativity breeds misery apathy and failure.

Life is full of challenges and it's how we deal with them that defines who we are and how successful we might become.

By the law of attraction we will bring into our lives people who mirror our own mental and emotional attitudes. If we mope and moan then it is entirely likely we will attract friends and colleagues who are equally down and dismal.

A positive mindset and a proactive 'can do' attitude will attract like-minded people into our lives.

Step Seven – It's not personal!
I know it can feel like a personal rejection when someone says no to the business or the product or service you are offering him or her. It isn't. The sooner you can understand that simple fact the easier your life in Network Marketing will be.

Remember from the previous step – adopting a positive mindset is essential.

**Every 'no' takes you a step closer
to the next 'yes'.**

And just because it is a 'no' now, it doesn't mean it is 'no' forever.

Chapter Two

If you keep doing the same thing then don't be surprised when you keep getting the same result.

Mum had been building a Network for ten years and was doing pretty well. But she worked the same way she had always done; face to face and on the telephone. She helped me to get going and I was content to let her run my business while I just did what she told me to do. I'm not a lazy person, so I don't really know why I was so inactive in those early days. I suppose I still didn't really buy into the business. She was so confident and competent and I was happy to follow her instructions. It never occurred to me to change or challenge how she worked. I had money coming in, which I welcomed, but the business still didn't really interest or excite me. Looking back, I can see that my failure to take ownership was a large part of the problem. Mum made it so easy for me. She knew exactly what she was doing, so why not let her lead the way? In those early days it never felt as though it was my business, more a subsidiary of hers. That was my fault for not fully engaging and for relying so heavily on her.

A tribute to her knowledge, experience and guidance, I found that simply by talking to my friends I was quickly promoted. Just five months after signing up, I received a second promotion and my earnings were around £500 per month. Of course, it was a snail's pace compared to what can be achieved with Social Media to help you in today's world of Network Marketing. But to me, it was all a bit of a surprise that I could be earning money like this from doing so little. It never occurred to me to do more. I had what I wanted, a bit of extra cash to help pay the bills and buy a few luxuries for the family.

I stayed at the same position in the marketing plan for the next eighteen months. Not exactly a flying start.

I was never a very confident person. In fact, in many ways I was painfully shy. Strange, since I had travelled all over the world, much of it on my own. So, in many ways I was a walking contradiction. In some ways I was mature and self-assured beyond my age. But to be told I would have to get up on stage and speak to a room full of people, I would disappear quicker than a spider faced with a fresh conker.

So when I saw my Mum stand up and speak at

a business presentation I felt incredibly proud. It was finally dawning on me that she was a serious player in a serious business and that actually, they weren't all middle-aged fuddy-duddies dabbling in sales.

'Hello, you must be Jan's girl,'

I turned my head and nodded at the lady smiling beside me.

'She's amazing, isn't she?'

I looked around the room; everyone's attention was focused on my mother. They were all listening, hanging on her every word. It was a bit like watching a stranger.

She finished speaking and the crowd applauded enthusiastically. The lady beside me nudged another woman and pointed to me.

'Jan's daughter…' she said, as though it were something to be very proud of.

As the second woman shook my hand warmly, I realised that while I, and my siblings, had never taken her business seriously at all. In the world of Network Marketing she was a well-respected person. I suppose we all take our parents for granted, in many ways still seeing them through the eyes of a child. Until that moment, I had never really thought about my mother as being anything other than my Mum. Of course, I knew she had a life beyond her parental boundaries, but I had never given it anything more than a passing thought. The fact that she was so well regarded, so accomplished, and surrounded by so many supportive friends and colleagues, really was a revelation to me.

'Well done,' I said, as soon as she re-joined me having to first weave her way through the room. She seemed to know everyone.

'Thanks,' she replied, smiling warmly at me. 'That'll be you one day.'

Talk about throw a bucket of cold water over someone. I shook my head so hard it hurt. No way. Never.

Mum nodded her head knowingly and left me to go and talk to one of her potential new team members.

I slid away to a quiet corner, the brief flash of enthusiasm and excitement draining away. I looked around the room; it wasn't for me. Sure,

I could do a little bit and create a small income. My eyes rested on the stage area where my mother had stood just a few minutes before. If moving up the marketing plan meant having to stand up and speak – well then, no, it was never going to be for me.

Of course, it had to change. I couldn't stay hiding behind my mother forever. As the business grew so did my confidence. I had to talk to individuals; including running planning meetings to help get new team members started. Then I had a few group sessions where I encouraged my down-line to share their success stories and tips. Eventually, the moment I had been dreading - I was asked to do a business presentation at the weekly local meeting.

'I can't.' I said to Mum, 'I feel physically sick just thinking about it.'

'I know,' she replied, 'I was just the same…'

'You were?'

'Of course! I thought, why would anyone want to listen to me? What could I possibly say that could inspire anyone?'

I remembered back to how proud I had felt the first time I saw her speak at a presentation. I remembered how the audience had listened to every word she had uttered. 'Do you still get nervous?'

'Always,' she said, putting the kettle on. 'Nerves can be a good thing, they keep you sharp and focused.'

'Really?' I replied doubtfully, 'I'm sure my mind turns to mush when I'm terrified.'

She placed a mug of tea on the table in front of me and sat down. 'What are you terrified of? What's the worst that can possibly happen when you stand up there to speak?'

I thought about it. I mentally placed myself in front of the crowd and let the fear run over me. 'I might not remember what to say, I can't speak at all, nobody listens to me…'

'Did you survive?'

I looked at her blankly.

'If your worst fears come true, does the experience harm you in any way?'

'Only my pride.'

'Well then,' she said with a shrug. 'You face the fear and do it anyway.'

So I did. My hands were trembling so much I couldn't hold my notes. I was sure that when I opened my mouth no words would come out, or even worse I might throw up. For a few seconds the fear paralysed me. I looked out into the audience, all silent, all attentive, all waiting for me to educate, to entertain and to enlighten them. Who was I kidding? I was a fraud, just a silly, scared woman who stumbled into the business because her mother kept pushing her to do so.

The words finally tumbled out. Not polished, not rehearsed or carefully crafted. But my simple story about how Network Marketing worked for me.

Somehow I managed to get through to the end and people applauded. I looked into the audience and saw my Mum wipe away a tear.

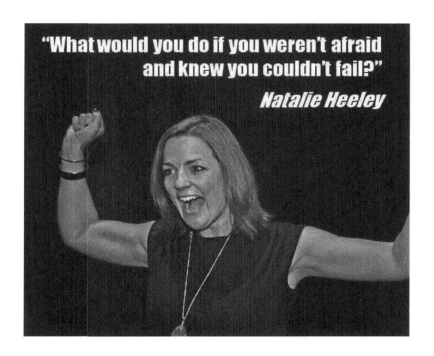

"What would you do if you weren't afraid and knew you couldn't fail?"

Natalie Heeley

I managed to smile and make my way out of the room and into the ladies cloakroom. I went into a stall, locked the door and let the tears fall. They were tears of relief. It was over; I had achieved the impossible and spoken in public. It was only a small gathering; maybe twenty or thirty people, but it was momentous to me. I had finally conquered the self-doubt and shyness that had been part of me for as long as I could remember.

I have never totally lost the nerves, but I learnt to accept them as part of the process. The flutter of butterflies in my belly became just part of the anticipation before a presentation. I never let the nerves control or restrict me. Just like my Mum says –

You face the fear and do it anyway.

My Story

How Facebook helped my in my business
By Claire Spencer

Prior to starting my business I was a child minder, which is well within my comfort zone. I thought, in the world of business – how could I network with a house full of 2 year-olds? So really, I hid behind Facebook for a long time, which I now know has had an effect on the growth of my business, but in turn has enabled me to become excellent at using it as one of many business tools.

In the early days it was easier to hide behind a status, because that was far less daunting than picking up the phone – this did however bring old school friends, past colleagues and people that had drifted from my life back into contact with me.

Over time my business grew rapidly. The success upped my confidence, which in turn led me to utilising many other methods of getting in front of people, leaving Facebook as a bolt on and not the only thing I do.

Now, Facebook is a great extension for me. It's how I showcase my lifestyle, people can follow me without physically having to follow me. I can have a personal image, my profile and a business image, my business page.

I have created a team support group, giving people a great community feeling. There are loads of resources, images and blogs to help my team develop their knowledge.

It's great for talking to groups of people using either the team group or messenger.

It's great for our prospects to have a look at what support we offer, dipping their toe in and taking a peek without having to commit.

We have customer support pages also, where they can share results, stories and ideas, we can also, as a team, support each other's customers.

Facebook is great as well because you can instantly change the information you're sharing, much easier than when you only have a website. You can literally create your branding and showcase what you want the world to see.

I recognise my teams' achievements and I showcase how I help my team by sharing photographs of training and events.

I post motivational messages regularly to inspire people out there who might be watching.

I use the messaging facility to chat to prospects, much like I would if I was out and about on my daily routine.

I can join groups that I am interested in to network with the fellow members and finally I can post adverts for my business and product with zero costs involved

Facebook is a great tool, when used in the right way. It is addictive, so make sure you put your phone, ipad and laptop down every once in a while and spend time with your family.

Over the last 5 years my life has gone from one of struggle, always running out of money before the end of the month and living with massive debt and a lifetime of child minding, to a business which now gives us a very healthy six figure income. My husband has left his career in project management, we have moved out of the town centre to the countryside, we have a beautiful home, the children are in fantastic new schools and we are totally debt free with a very healthy nest egg growing each and every month.

Network Marketing has taken me out of my comfort zone and given me self-confidence, financial freedom and a better, more secure future for my family.

Chapter Three

Make your children the reason...

My business was ticking along; I had an extra income of around £500 per month. Enough money to buy those little extras that make life easier. I was complacent and content to be at home with Will and Rosie. It was important to me that I had time to spend with them, I didn't want to be out working full time, missing each milestone as they grew up. In all honesty, looking back, if someone had said to me 'you need to work harder and take your business to the next level.' I would have used the same reason that I hear again and again.

'I can't. I have two young children.'

It's a valid point, isn't it? I have nothing but admiration for the full-time mothers and fathers who get up at the crack of dawn, run around getting themselves and the children ready to drop at nursery or school. They do a long, hard day at work, then pick the children up again, spend a snatched hour or so of quality time with their offspring after dinner and before bedtime. Weekends they play catch up with the housework and the shopping, while trying to fit in activities and adventures for the children. Of course, it's easier with a helpful, supportive partner but, for a single mum or dad, life is all about earning a living to support the family. The same family, that they are now too exhausted to fully enjoy.

It is so hard to earn an income and still have the time and energy to enjoy each day. We all dream of being rich enough to do what we want, without having to spend every day working to pay the bills. But dreams are just that and, unless you happen to have a fairy god mum or the odd Genie hiding under the bed, they rarely come true.

We get so set on the conventional path that we accept it as the only way to live. We park our dreams in some dusty corner of our minds and hope that one day we will win the lottery.

I was the same. I settled for what I had. I didn't look beyond the day and into the future because I knew that the things I wanted were beyond my grasp. A private school education for my children, travel and holidays like I had enjoyed as a child. A nice house and enough money to not have to worry if an unexpected bill lands on the carpet. Of course, for most of us that longed-for lottery win never comes and we have to manage each day as best as we can. Moving from one financial crisis to the next; dreading the mail bringing more bills and wishing that payday wasn't still two weeks away.

At this stage in my life I had already been told about Dream Books and about setting goals. But I thought about them in the same way as I did the fairy stories. Without the fairy dust they were simply never going to work.

And then one day everything changed.

It didn't seem like a special day. It was dull and overcast, one of those heavy, grey days that England does so well. Rosie was just a little tot and Will was at his pre-school. I've no idea where the morning disappeared to. I remember I had a machine full of washing and spent five minutes debating whether or not to risk hanging it out on the line. Or should I shove it in the tumble dryer and pay the price? I did spend thirty minutes making business calls while my daughter had her nap and another thirty minutes tidying up the trail of toys and crumbs that seem to follow small children wherever they go.

**So nothing exceptional.
Nothing out of the ordinary.**

**Just another typical morning in my
unremarkable and uneventful life.**

Rosie and I turned up at the pre-school to
collect Will. We waited at the door with the
other mums, along with one or two dads and
an occasional grandparent. Hoping the skies
didn't decide that now was the perfect time
to deposit their heavy loads. I'd forgotten my
umbrella and didn't fancy getting drenched.

I exchanged a few polite hellos and the typical British discussion about the weather and
eventually the door opened and we all piled in
to find and collect our little darlings. Will was
gathering up his things and his teacher caught
my eye. I smiled and, encouraged, she came
closer and glancing at my son she said, 'Will is
so excited about going to Disney.'

I thought for a moment that she must have
mistaken me for someone else. She had the
wrong parent or the wrong child. What was she
talking about? I looked around to see if it was
even me she was speaking too. Given the fact
that she was staring straight at me with a big
grin on her face I had to conclude that it was.

'We took our girls last year. They loved it, I'm sure you'll have a wonderful time.'

'Disney,' I said, still not really understanding what was going on.

'Yes, Will said he's going to see Buzz Light-year.'

It was starting to make sense. The TV was full of adverts for Disney and Will always became very animated when he saw his favourite toy was a life size character complete with ray gun, posing with excited children.

'Are you going to Florida or Disneyland Paris?'

Will came running over to me and I bent down to hug him. His teacher was called away to sort out a squabble over matching Lazy Town lunchboxes and I was saved having to make up an answer for her.

But that's when it struck me – that moment when the light bulb flashes on in your mind and the penny finally drops. They might both be clichés, but that doesn't mean they are not true. It is when the fog and the clouds of every-day life suddenly clear and a simple truth is revealed.

I realised that I was kidding myself, thinking that I had everything I wanted. That £500 per month was enough and my life was exactly as I wanted it to be. It simply wasn't true.

My son wanted to go to Disney. He wanted to meet his hero, Buzz, and have an exciting holiday. How could I deprive him of his dream? I knew then, at that moment, that I had to find a way to make it happen.

His dream became my goal.

For the first time in my life I actually sat down and filled in the first page of my Dream Book.

TAKE WILL AND ROSIE TO DISNEY

A dream is only a starting point. To turn it into reality you need to turn it into a goal and from there you need a plan to make it happen. I rang my mother and told her what had happened.

'We can't afford it,' I said, 'I need to earn more money.'

'That's all right,' she replied, 'anything is possible. Come round and we will plan it together.'

So, the next day I went to my Mum's house. We took a hard look at my business and between us we devised a strategy to basically give it (and me) a kick up the backside.

I did my research into Disneyland Paris and discovered that January was the cheapest time to go. I made the decision that it was going to happen. I took a deep breath and a determined leap of faith. I went ahead and booked the holiday, paying on my credit card.

**Suddenly it all seemed possible.
It's amazing what a mixture of
motivation, positive goal setting
and proactive action can do.**

Later that evening I told the children, 'after Christmas we are going to Disney...'

I didn't even get to finish the sentence before Will was dancing around the kitchen with excitement. I'm not sure what my husband thought. I think 'crazy' was probably somewhere in his head. We couldn't afford it, not if things stayed the same. So, the only answer was to make changes. And I did. I started taking my business seriously. I realised that it had been a bit of a hobby, a side-line that gave us extra money each month, but wasn't a 'proper' job. My attitude and perception had to change. It was time to get serious.

**Instead of my children being
an excuse not to do the business.
They became my reason for doing it.**

I gave Will the Dream Book. I stuck pictures of Disney inside it and every time my motivation faltered I picked the book up and reminded myself why I had to make the call or go out and help a new recruit to launch their business.

Will ran around showing everyone who came to the house my Dream Book. 'Mummy works so we can go to Disney,' he told the window cleaner.

With my new determination to push my business forward I followed up on my son's first contact and handed the bemused man a pack of free samples, a promotional leaflet and my business card. Of course, now I would connect to him via Facebook, but that wasn't an option back then, the potential of social media was unknown.

How to use your phone and Facebook to connect with a potential new team member

If I was trying to interest the window cleaner (or anyone else) in the business now, this is what I would do at first contact.

I would hand them my phone with my Facebook account open and I would ask them to find their profile and send a friend request from me to them.

Next time they log on to their Facebook page they can accept my friend request and we will be connected.

Of course, if they have their phone handy at our first encounter they can log straight in to Facebook and add me immediately.

I would then take a screenshot of their Facebook page so that I don't forget who they are and I remember to follow up.

Once we are connected I can private message them with a link to a promotional video that will introduce the company and the business plan to them.

This approach is very effective and replaces the exchange of business cards. Not only does it mean that I don't have to spend a lot of time talking about the company, and the opportunity, but it allows him/her to discover for themselves, via the link, in the comfort of their own home. Add to that the fact that they now have my Facebook feed which is always focused on positive messages and lifestyle. If it's not right for them now chances are I will be a constant reminder of what is on offer.

Try it – it works!

Within two months of setting my target I had attained promotion and a 5% pay increase. Disney was no longer a distant dream; it was an easily attainable goal.

I had finally realised the power and potential of Network Marketing and how I could use it to benefit my family.

It wasn't all dreams and happy ever afters. Life is always about hurdles to be jumped and disappointments to be overcome. Our trip to Disney was almost lost when a series of delays, mishaps and a massive accident on the motorway made us miss our slot on the Eurotunnel train.

'But we're only a couple of minutes late,' I pleaded with the man at the gate who controlled the barrier and was preventing us from driving onto the train. He had clearly heard it all before.

'Sorry, but the gate is shut ready for departure.'

Panic had already chased me all the way to Folkestone as I fought the traffic and willed time to slow down and allow us to make it to the train. In the rear view mirror, I could see my two children in the back of the car. Will was already picking up on the atmosphere, not surprising since I was doing a poor job of hiding it. He was clutching his Buzz Lightyear toy and I could see the worry in his serious young eyes. Luckily Rosie was sleeping and therefore oblivious when it finally got too much for me and I burst into tears.

The gatekeeper, desperate to get rid of me, and my soggy tissue, sent us over to the supervisor's hut and my mother, who was dealing with the situation much better than I was, got us booked onto the next train.

'You'll have to change at Paris, this one doesn't go straight through to Euro Disney.' The supervisor told us.

I didn't care. I could have hugged her.

'That's fine,' my mother said calmly, although I knew she was as relieved as I was.

We finally arrived a couple of hours later than expected, but it didn't matter. None of it mattered once we knew we were finally at Disney. Rosie was a bit scared by some of the characters, but she loved the Princesses and Will got his photo with Buzz. We all enjoyed the fantastic Electrical Parade, photos were taken and memories created. The next few days were magical for my children and I knew that I would never again doubt the power of a Dream Book or the importance of goal setting.

It's not just about knowing what you want – you need to know why you want it.

**My children became my reason for
doing the business rather than
my excuse for doing nothing.**

How to create a Dream Book

Having a visual stimulant makes your mind
believe you have achieved your goal before
you really have. Looking at it everyday will

help you and motivate you to do the necessary activity to achieve it. Because your mind can visually see it, the law of attraction will bring it into your life.

With experience, you can just shut your eyes and see, touch and taste your goals and dreams, but to do this you need to train your mind with the visual stimulant.

I was told by my sponsor to do this for a long time - but I thought it was like a school activity and didn't understand how some pictures on a board or book would help me.

It wasn't until my son, Will, wanted to go to Disney that I finally tried it and made it work for me.

So, how do you build a dream book?

Step One – Know what you want and why you want it.
Think about what you have accomplished already in life. What are you most proud of? You need to understand what matters most to you and what motivates you to achieve it.

Step Two – Touch an emotion, make it matter
If you can create a Dream Book that has an emotional impact on you it will be much easier

for you to achieve. For me, it's all about my children. They are my emotional why.

Step Three – Make it a family affair
From producing my first Dream Book I understood the power of involving your loved ones in the process. Make it a family activity so your partner and children can understand why you need to go out and work, because they too can see the goals and dreams and be part of the journey with you and not become resentful of you working.

Step Four – Create the goals
Write a list of 30-50 things you want for you and your family in the next 10 years. It may be financial or it might be emotional. Don't limit yourself to physical achievements. You might want to develop more personal qualities – to be a more patient person, for example.

Step Five – Create a Timeline
Now, put a time line on them   - what do you want in the next 3 month, 6 months, 12 months, 3 years, 5 years and 10 years.

Without a timeline goals are just dreams.

You need to put a time on it, create a deadline to work too. Then you can work towards achieving each goal.

Sometimes we get it wrong, Things change, our dreams and desires shift and the goals might need to be adjusted. View your long-term goal as the postcode in your life's satnav. You want it to take you on the most direct route to your destination. Your short-term goals are stops along the way. Occasionally, you might have to make a diversion and find another route. There will always be unforeseen disruptions and challenges in your business and personal life. It is all part of building a business. You have to be flexible and willing to adapt. But, if you don't have a destination, an aim, a goal, a dream, then how do you know which way to travel?

Step Six – Visualise your achievements
Close your eyes and see yourself in the future. What could your life be like once you achieve the goals you are setting for yourself? Picture how your life will really look. What can you see around you? Who are you with? Regardless of whether your goal is material or emotional you need to be able to visualise yourself in the future, like watching a movie in your mind that is your own creation.

Step Seven – Plan your next twelve months
Consider what you want to achieve in the next six months and the next twelve months. Make them the stepping-stones towards your long-term destination. It is very hard to stay motivated when the goal is for five or ten year's time. So you need to entice and encourage yourself with smaller, achievable steps that ultimately will lead you to fulfilling your life's

dreams and ambitions. If you want to be a concert pianist then you know you will have to practice hard and work hard. You can't simply walk on stage and start playing with no knowledge, no training or expertise. What you would need to do is start at the beginning. Your first goal might be to have lessons and pass the first piano exam. Then, progress through the lessons until you reach a proficient level. Next, you might need to find a more specialised instructor in order to increase your competency levels. Your stepping stone goal might be to play for the first time in public, maybe in a small setting to a friendly audience. Eventually, step-by-step, you can work your way up to achieving the long-term goal of becoming a concert pianist.

It is exactly the same with your personal and business goals. You set out with a long term plan and then fill the space from starting point to destination with smaller steps. Each goal achieved along the way is a valuable lesson learnt or a new skill acquired. Keep visualising the future you want and keep your mind focused on your ultimate goal and eventually that is where you will end up.

Step Eight – Define what you want the most
Choose the most important goals that you

have set yourself - the four that sum up what you want from your life. Write down how the attainment of them will change your life and how you might feel when you achieve them. Close your eyes and let your imagination fully embrace this wonderful new future. If you have set the right goals this process should touch you emotionally and fire your motivation and excitement. Dare to dream and then turn those dreams into a life plan. This can be an emotional moment. You need to truly care and to connect to the vision of your future.

Step Nine – Share your Dream Book
If you are building a network marketing team, organise a get together. Those who have already created a dream book can share their dreams and plans and those who have not yet taken the step can be encouraged and inspired to work on their own.

Encourage everyone to be bold and brave. A goal shouldn't be easy. It should challenge and stretch you. Share your dream book and your goals with your up-line, down-line and side-line. Make your Dream Book the window that looks into your future. Share that vision with the people around you. If you keep the Dream Book secret then it makes it easy for you to give up at the first set back. By telling everyone what you want to achieve you are reinforcing the message and making yourself account-able.

Have fun with your team. Make it an event and write your own dream board to show how it's done. Supply lots of magazines for cutting out images. Have coloured pens, scissors and glue and post-it notes.

Step Ten – Understand the law of attraction.
One of my Mentor's, the wonderful Dave O'Connor, taught me the power of the theatre of your own mind. I can close my eyes and see my future – every detail of how I want it to be. You need to understand that you can attract into your life whatever elements you want. You simply need to want it enough and be physically and emotionally committed. Be prepared to keep focused on your goals and fill your mind with positive thoughts and promises.

Don't just set goals that are easy to achieve. You should always have some that scare you and push you out of your comfort zone.

Life is an adventure. Don't just be a spectator, full of disappointments and regrets. Go out and engage and enjoy.

DARE TO DREAM

Chapter Four

Believe in yourself

Even before the Disney trip I was aware of a slow disenchantment creeping over me. My marriage was in trouble. Our relationship wasn't working anymore. However, it wasn't a reality I was prepared to face up to. My own parents splitting up during my teenage years made me determined never to put my own children though the same pain.

But sometimes, staying is the wrong choice for the children too. I didn't want Will and Rosie to grow up in a family where they were the only thing holding it all together. I didn't believe the children needed that kind of pressure, nor did I believe it was a good message for them to live with. When they grew up and became adults, I wanted them to go out and find partners they could love and be happy with. Bringing them up in a household that put up with less simply didn't seem right to me.

My husband was a good father and a kind man, but we had grown apart and we wanted different things from life. Our aspirations and ambitions were so wide apart that we were in danger of it all tumbling into a chasm. The bridge that united us was crumbling and I knew that the marriage couldn't survive for much longer.

I decided to throw myself into the business. It offered a focus and a bit of escapism from my marriage. As a result of my work and attention, the income slowly started to grow. I realised that I could be happy alone, as a single parent. I needed to work harder and build the income so that I could support the kids. I didn't want any family split to affect them financially. I knew that I couldn't protect them from all the fallout that divorce would inevitably bring, but at least I could make sure that we had enough money coming in. So I worked incredibly hard to ensure our financial stability.

It worked. I experienced a whirlwind year in the business. Suddenly, I was zooming up the charts and my income went from £800 per month to £4566. Everyone watched in amazement and as a result I found myself inundated by potential new team members. Seeing what I had achieved in just 10 months everyone, not surprisingly, wanted to be a part of it. Such speedy climbs were quite unheard of back then, so I caused quite a stir within the company.

In 2009 I made the painful decision to ask for a divorce. My self-esteem, never terribly high, plummeted to an all time low and I found myself facing the saddest, hardest, most miserable time of my life.

I had failed. My greatest wish was for my children to be happy and secure and I hadn't even been able to give them that.

'You have a right to happiness as well.' Mum said, trying to comfort me on a particularly down day.

'This doesn't feel like happiness.'

She sat down beside me and took my hand. 'It will get better.'

I looked at her and thought back to when I was sixteen. Is this what she went through? All that time that I was blaming her for breaking up our family. Was she consumed with worry and self-doubt?

'What did you do to make it better?' I asked.

She smiled and stood up to open a bottle of wine. 'I threw myself into my business.'

Would that work for me? I had no motivation and no confidence left. How could I go out and sell a marketing plan when I felt so low?

The business was still ticking along and supporting us. It had already proved its potential and surpassed any of my expectations. Also, it had allowed me to show what I was capable of achieving for myself. So why was I struggling so much now? All that hard- earned self-confidence had deserted me.

Just getting the children up and ready for school was a massive effort for me. As soon as I dropped them off and kissed them good-bye, the tears would start and I would walk home, half -blinded with soggy eyes and snotty nose. I hated how I was and then I hated myself for not being strong enough to fight it. In the end I turned to professional help. I went to counselling and my doctor prescribed me anti-depressants. I never took them. I put the pills in my bedside drawer and regarded them as my safety net. They were there, ready and available. They were comforting and terrifying at the same time. The Doctor said I needed them and I certainly felt more miserable than I had ever felt in my life. But I was scared to take them. Afraid that, if I started I would never break free and a cycle of depression and drugs would become my reality.

The worst time was when Will and Rosie went to their Dad's for the weekend and the time stretched ahead of me and I was shrouded in dark thoughts and loneliness. I knew I had to somehow change my perception and turn the darkness and negativity into something positive.

**I owed it to my children to
find a different way of thinking.**

I tried really hard to make the business my pathway back to happiness. But my total lack of confidence held me back. It felt as though some invisible force had pulled the plug and all my self worth and get up and go had drained away.

Not that anyone who knew me back then would have a clue what I was going through. As a naturally private person I didn't want to admit I needed help and told no one about my counselling sessions. I put on the Natalie Heeley happy mask and buried my emotions. Tears were only allowed when nobody was around to see them. I felt a bit like an actor in a play. I was saying the words and playing the part, pretending that I was the character I was portraying, but underneath a very different person was struggling to survive.

I've heard it said that a crisis, although precipitated by a traumatic event, often has its origins in something lodged in our past. There comes a time when memories hidden away need to be pulled out, examined, dealt with and then discarded.

Of course, everyone is different and every person's pain and depression derives from a different circumstance. I think for me it was the overwhelming feeling of failure and uselessness that paralysed me with misery.

Depression is a terrible thing.
Destructive and self-perpetuating.

My Mum was worrying about me, the children were picking up on the negative aura that shrouded me. I had to find a way forward.

For me, facing the past was the first step. Beginning with the anger and resentment from my own parents' break-up. Until I stopped to really think about where all my hurt was coming from. I had no idea I still carried these feelings around. If anyone had asked I would have said that it was all in the past and I was completely over it. Clearly, that wasn't true. So I went to my Mum and talked it through with her. For the first time we really talked about that difficult time in both our lives and more importantly, I listened.

I also allowed myself to mentally return to a past romance and a boyfriend who, as a successful professional footballer, had completely overshadowed me. He lived his life in the media spotlight while I hovered in the shadows.

It occurred to me that what a contradiction my personality was. One part of me was strong, resilient, and confident enough to literally take on the world. I travelled alone across several continents with little money and limited language skills. Yet the flip side of me was this shy, timid shadow that would happily don an invisibility cloak and remain hidden forever.

Maybe I had a split personality? Or maybe I was allowing the wrong part of me to rule the other. Maybe it was time for me to choose.

Did I want to be Natalie the strong or Natalie the invisible?

I made the decision to be the former. I didn't transform overnight and the depression lingered for many months. But, with the help of family, the motivation to do my best for the children, the support of a growing network, the diversion of a fun business and the change in my own mental attitude I managed to become the woman I wanted to be.

How to build your self-belief

Step one – Let go of the past.
We all have baggage. Upsets and disappointments that can make us jaded or cynical. Often we cling onto the feelings of resentment and pain. We keep them close and relive them whenever we want to indulge in a dose of the POM's (poor old me syndrome) We carry the past around like a physical scar from a cut and often find it hard to let go. Everything that happens to us, good or bad, is an opportunity to learn, to grow and to move forward. Our past helps to shape us, but it doesn't have to control us. Decide the person you want to be, the positive attributes you want to have and then determine to make it happen.

An old man talks to his grandson about life. 'Inside us all a battle rages between two wolves.' He says. 'One is evil - he is anger, envy, sorrow, regret, greed, arrogance, self-pity, guilt, resentment, inferiority, lies, false pride, superiority, and ego. But the other wolf is good - he is joy, peace, love, hope, serenity, humility, kindness, benevolence, empathy, generosity, truth, compassion, and faith.'

The boy considers the words for a minute before turning to his grandfather, 'which wolf will win?' he asks.

The old man looks calmly back at the boy and replies, 'whichever one you feed.'

If you struggle with the negative voice that whispers in your ear, then borrow the belief that your mentor/up-line has in you until you have built up enough belief and confidence in yourself.

I used to visualise my negativity with a mini-me on one shoulder whispering, 'I can't do this.'

But my mentor Jayne, would be on the other shoulder saying, 'yes you can.'

STRONG INVISIBLE

Which one are you going to feed?

Which one are you going to feed?

We can all be the person we want to be. Let go of all the negatives that hold us back and move into the future full of positive energy and self-belief.

Step Two – Let Social Media lead the way

Nothing builds confidence as fast as success. Facebook and other Social Media formats allow you to build your business without having to make phone calls or deal with people face to face until you feel ready. For some people, especially those who are shy or lacking in self-confidence this is a great way to get started. (See chapter nine for a master class in social media) When I was at my lowest ebb, I could hide behind my online persona. Natalie on Facebook was always smiling, always confident and always encouraging, proactive and positive. Eventually, all that great energy touched the physical me and played a part in getting me through that terrible time.

Step Three – Feed your mind

Positive people keep their minds focused on positive thoughts. Read inspirational books, listen to uplifting stories, watch encouraging training videos, and mix with like-minded people.

Step Four – Mingle and socialise

I know this is a tough one when you suffer from low self-esteem or lack self-belief. Take it step by step. Use whatever meetings, training and development opportunities your network has on offer. You will soon find that mixing with other people who share your Network Marketing world will give you confidence.

Step Five – Support from your Mentors
I was lucky in the business because I had my Mum to mentor me through the early days of building my business. Later on, I was helped and encouraged by the top couple in the company Jayne and John. They taught me so much, giving me their time, the benefit of their experience and sharing their belief in the business and in me. I was also helped by a very special and successful lady from another Network, who, like my mother, was called Jan. But the person who probably helped me develop personally more than any other was Dave O'Connor. I call him my mind-set Guru and he taught me about the importance of a positive mind-set, goal setting and self-belief. I don't believe I could have had the success I have achieved today without the help of my many mentors. Don't be afraid to ask for help and encouragement. Network Marketing thrives on mutual respect and support. If you don't get what you need from your immediate up-line then look beyond them. Someone in the business will be willing to help you.

Step Six – Pass it on

I love seeing others succeed. I pass on everything I can that I think can benefit my downline. I post positivity via Facebook and on-line support and encouragement through You Tube training videos. There's nothing like a post to recognise people as they progress along their journey. I encourage them via Facebook groups, right from their very first steps. It helps to build their belief in themselves very quickly.

I also like to use live webinar sessions to shout out some recognition. Everyone likes to know the effort they are putting in is noticed and appreciated. Often, those being recognized, share their story on the webinar, which gradually helps to build up their own confidence towards being a great trainer themselves.

I speak at meetings and still do as many individual business-building sessions that I can fit in. I run webinars and make sure that I connect with my Network in every way I can. Nothing builds confidence as quickly as the buzz you get from helping someone else strive towards his or her goals.

Chapter Five

Surround yourself with positive, uplifting people

Throughout my dark days I felt very alone. I was lucky enough to have family and friends who all did their best to help and support me. Difficult for them, since I never really confided in anyone. Those closest to me only knew I was going through a rough patch and no doubt they believed I was adjusting to the divorce. Which was true enough, but they had no idea how deep my depression went, nor were they aware of the panic attacks that would suddenly and randomly grip me.

The business helped me, as did my children and my family, but I couldn't have rebuilt myself without intensive intervention by Dave O'Connor.

Dave came into my life when he offered his services to the Network Company my business is with. One of my Up-line mentors arranged (with no idea of my need) for me to be a guinea pig. He wanted five volunteers to work with for twenty-one days – apparently the time it takes to form a habit. Feeling I had nothing to lose and potentially everything to gain I embraced the opportunity.

I was very open to the idea of personal and emotional development and so at 9am every morning, I participated in a conference call with Dave and the other guinea pigs.

I found it incredibly helpful and I stuck with his instructions long after the sessions had finished. He became my mentor and eventually a friend. He made me a 'how to cope' recording which I listened to every night when I went to bed. I have no doubt at all that his words, his encouragement and the self-development tools he taught me, were more useful to me than anything my Doctor could have offered.

As my shattered self-belief began to grow, so did my business.

I began to realise that it's not what happens to us that defines who we are, but rather, how we deal with it.

Anyone who is serious about building a business must also be aware of his or her own personal development as well.

As my life began to improve I found myself

wishing I had someone to share it with. I started to socialise more and even went on a few dates. Although none of these dates went anywhere it was great to be back out in the world and living rather than hiding away indoors.

There was a man who had been in my life for a very long time. Gladstone was a close family friend, some years older than me and, as a teenager I used to babysit his children.

Like me he was divorced, but remained on amicable terms with his ex-wife. I had remained in contact with all of them including the children who were now adults themselves. I am Godmother to his daughter and so he would drop her off or pick her up after a sleepover at my house. Sometimes he would stay for a little while and we would chat and on a couple of occasions he supplied me with a friendly shoulder to cry on. As someone I had known for so long and trusted completely, he was one of the few people who ever knew how very unhappy I had been at times.

It came as no surprise when I was invited to his 50th birthday party in London. It was a great evening and the alcohol flowed freely. I ended up more than a little bit tipsy along with almost everyone else there. At some point during the evening, Gladstone decided that my single state was unacceptable and tried to set me up with one of his mates. Although I never actually dated his friend, we did sit and chat over a few drinks during the party. It was good to flirt and have some fun.

During that time Gladstone and I talked more frequently and our friendship grew. He was always such an easy man to be around. I don't know if it was because I had known him for so long or maybe it was the age gap, but whatever the reason, I found myself totally at ease with him. As a successful professional cricket player, I found him inspirational. I liked his energy, his determination and ambition. Yet, despite his success he was not arrogant. I looked forward to our telephone and text chats. His opinion was one that I valued, he never put me down, but he was always honest and willing to offer supportive advice.

I was invited to another birthday celebration. His son's twenty first family dinner. I was honoured for me to be asked, and excited to be going. I always got on well with the family and couldn't believe that the little kid I had looked after all those years ago was all grown up. I also liked the fact that despite the divorce some years earlier they could all still get together as a family complete with Gladstone's ex's new partner.

The dinner went well with lots of wine, good conversation and laughter. It was a lovely restaurant, dimly lit and with an ambient atmosphere. I felt more relaxed and happy than I had for a long time. I sipped my coffee and Gladstone caught my eye from across the table.

'Fancy going on somewhere?' he said quietly.

I smiled back and nodded. 'I'll get my coat.'

I'm not sure, looking back, if I knew at that moment where we were heading. I probably did on some sub-conscience level. Later on in the evening, when he bent his head and gently kissed my lips, I was warm and ready for the contact. I don't think either of us had seen it coming, but equally, neither of us was surprised. Our friendship had been slowly growing into something stronger. When the romance finally happened it immediately felt right, like arriving home after a long and arduous journey.

It felt as though all the areas of my life were

finally pulling together. Of course, I'd heard the saying 'Success Breeds Success,' but never really understood it until then. I realise now that it is all about perception. If you are in a dark, negative place then those are the vibes that you send out to the world. Who wants to work with someone who is miserable, depressed and failing? A positive change in attitude can turn everything around. Not overnight, but over time. If you want your life to change for the better then it has to start with you.

I'm sure that it was no coincidence that my most successful years in business have come since I've been in a happy, supportive relationship.

Dare to dream - visualise your emotional, physical and environmental state not as it is, but as you want it to be.

Set goals – big ones, small ones, long term and short term. Drag yourself out of your comfort zone.

**Make a dream book –
show it, share it, believe it.**

Feed your brain - Read inspirational and informative stories. Listen to positive messages from development CD's. Watch training videos.

Mix and Mingle – Go to meetings. Mix with positive people. Surround yourself with people who share your aspirations. Nothing destroys dreams quicker than negative people. I don't mean you can't allow a touch of reality into your life, but don't let other people drag you down.

Negative people focus on the problems while positive people focus on finding solutions.

Support and be Supportive – Train and be trained. Never stop learning. Listen to other people, share experiences and tips. Pass on whatever works for you to your down-line. Network Marketing is at its best when everyone is mutually supportive.

We all want to be happy and healthy. We all dream of financial stability and try to give our children the best start in life that we can. Nobody has an easy path. Everyone has hurdles to jump and some have mountains to climb. It is so often the case that those who seem to do well, carry on and do even better. Those who slip into a downward spiral seem to slide further and further into despair. Bad luck, bad timing, bad genetics and bad company – all can play a part in a person's misfortune. Nobody can avoid a rocky path completely. But if you change your mental attitude then you can change your luck and your life. We take in what we reflect out.

Decide that from this moment on that every rock that makes you stumble and slows your path to success will be dealt with, learnt from and moved aside. We only learn through experience. Don't let a difficulty or setback be a failure. If you do something that doesn't give you the reward you wanted, view it as a lesson learnt. Either you change how you did it before or you look for another way to achieve the objective.

Every No is a step closer to a Yes.

Every set back is a lesson learned that takes you closer to your goal attainment.

Imagine being a top footballer. How many times do you think they practice in front of a goalpost and kick the ball? Do you think every time they miss or the Goalie deflects or catches the ball, they fall to the ground in despair and give up playing football forever? No, of course they don't. They practice to learn and improve their game and skills. Every time they kick the ball and miss, their mind and all their senses register what went wrong and come up with new strategies and solutions to do it better at the next attempt.

You are no different to the footballer. You might not be kicking a ball, but you are working and learning and your aim is to achieve your goal.

Be positive and positive people will come into your life.

Treat every setback as a lesson to be learnt.

Learn the lesson and do better next time.

Chapter Six

Sometimes we all need a bit of help

Running a business and being a single mum was seriously challenging at times. Things were going really well and my Network was growing rapidly. Which meant juggling work and family was becoming much more difficult. I tried several solutions, including an Au Pair, babysitters and child-minders. I felt guilty and worried about Will and Rosie whenever I was working late or away from home. It was a difficult balance.

I had a taste of success and had found some ambition.

I wanted to prove to myself and to everyone else that I could achieve something wonderful. I needed to be the best that I could be. I wasn't striving to be Number One in the business for recognition, but I wanted everything that position would give me in terms of lifestyle, security and financial freedom. I had dreams and a desire to give my children everything I possibly could, including a private-school education. I felt that schools had changed a lot since I was a child and not necessarily for the best. I wanted the smaller classes and the extra opportunities that private schools could offer. I had heard horror stories about failing pupils and falling standards at state schools. Of course, I knew that for every bad experience there were probably a hundred positive, happy ones. But I wasn't comfortable with what was on offer, I knew I wanted more for Will and Rosie. A feeling reinforced by a friend who was a teacher at a private school, she was always so positive and enthusiastic.

I felt the most valuable thing I could do for my kids was to give them the very best education available. Surely that would set them up for whatever future they might choose for themselves.

I now had the skills and mind-set to turn those dreams into goals and plans, but somehow I now had to find a balance between family time and working the business. It wasn't always easy to achieve.

I now understood that anything was possible.

I also understood that often in life there is a price to pay if we want to stretch beyond the confines of our ordinary lives. I knew I wanted to be the best that I could be. I wanted to earn the big money and secure a great future for my children. One of my mentors, John told me that if I worked my butt off for five years I could then slow down and be financially secure for the rest of my life.

It was an idea that had seemed totally impossible before, but one that I now bought in to completely. I wanted that security for my family and I wasn't afraid of hard work.

I just had to find a way to make it happen.

The children were really good. The pressure was more my own, internal guilt than any complaints from them. I spent every minute I could with my children and made sure that they reaped the benefits from the business. The Dream Book was a huge help because we complied each new page as a family so they always had a very visual reminder as to why the child-minder had picked them up from school or the Au Pair was cooking dinner.

Being as I loved travel so much I was keen to pass on that same passion to my children. A lot of the Dream Book was filled with places we all wanted to go to. I made a point of booking time off during school holidays so that we could go away and reap the rewards of all my hard work.

I also involved the children in my success.

They knew all about the business and they understood why I did it. Whenever I achieved a new level or secured a big bonus we celebrated as a family. They sometimes came with me to events and conferences and they were with me on stage when I collected the first of my big bonus cheques.

'When will we get a bigger one, Mummy?' Will whispered as I clutched the large, fake cheque and we watched other Networkers collect ones with more noughts on the end than mine.

'Soon,' I replied, determined to make it so. I knew that the faster I climbed the ladder the sooner my aims and ambitions for financial security would be a reality. Nature or nurture, clearly my son had the same view!

Childcare was an on-going issue, but I kept going and somehow we muddled through.

'You're over doing it, Nat,' Mum said, early one evening. She had popped over to see the children after school and stayed for dinner. 'You look exhausted.'

'I'm fine,' I smiled, although I knew she was right. People coped with just a few hours sleep all the time. Hadn't Margaret Thatcher survived with four hours a night, topped up with the occasional power nap? And she ran an entire country. I refused to let lack of sleep interfere with my climb to the top or with the time I spent with Will and Rosie.

'How can I help?' she asked, clearly not buying my 'bright and breezy' mask at all.

'Magic me up a few extra hours in the day please.' I quipped lightly, opening a bottle of wine and pouring myself a glass. I half filled a glass for Mum and handed it to her.

She took the wine and allowed herself to be diverted by Rosie who was keen to show her the new Disney Princess doll she had saved up for and bought.

Despite plenty of holidays and fun days out I still insisted the children learnt the value of money. They were encouraged to save for things they wanted and pocket money was only topped up on birthdays or at Christmas, and as a reward for some good deed or achievement. Anything material they wanted outside of normal 'present' events, I expected them to save up for and pay at least half for. Whenever I received my bonus cheque I gave them pocket money so that they felt the benefits of the business in the same way as I did. I also paid 10% from every bonus divided into each of their savings accounts for when they reach eighteen.

I sat down on the sofa and closed my eyes briefly. I could hear the children laughing upstairs with their Granny. The tiredness I had been fighting for months must have gotten the better of me because when I opened my eyes again it was dark and I had a soft, fleecy blanket draped over me.

I looked around and realised that I must have been asleep for a couple of hours. I pushed the blanket off and stood up far too quickly. I had to pause to steady myself as dizziness hit me. I felt disorientated and faint. I knew it was only a blood rush caused by jumping up too quickly, but still I felt as though it was my body issuing me a warning. Even though I didn't want to face it, Mum was right, as usual, and I was clearly overdoing it.

I felt as though I had little choice.

By this stage I totally believed that you could have anything you want in life so long as you are prepared to pay the price required to achieve it.

'Better?' Mum asked, walking into the lounge. 'You were sound asleep.'

'Guess I was a bit tired,' I replied, folding up the blanket.

'Will and Rosie are in bed.' Mum said.

I looked at her, surprised, it was even later than I thought. 'Are they all right?'

'Good as gold.' She smiled, 'although I think I was tricked. They both insisted that you always read two chapters from the book…'

'You were definitely had, I only ever read one.'

She grinned, 'I don't mind, I love having them.' She walked into the hall and picked her coat up from the hanger. 'Better get going.'

I waved as she drove away, 'drive carefully,' I called out. It was dark and late and she had almost an hour's drive in front of her. I closed the door and walked back into the lounge, sat down and checked my phone. As I scrolled down the Facebook notifications and read my emails I found I wasn't really concentrating. An idea was beginning to form. A simple solution that seemed so perfect I was struggling to believe it could be true.

I had to wait an hour before I could make the call and then I added on an extra five minutes to let Mum get indoors and put the kettle on. Time usually raced for me, but that evening it felt as though it had slowed down to a snail's pace. Eventually it was time. I started to press speed dial but before I could make the call my phone rang and it was Mum calling me.

'Pack up and move closer…' she said, before I even had time to say hello. 'It's the perfect solution. I can help with the children, you get your extra hours and best of all I get to spend more time with my grandkids.'

'Yes.' I said.

'I know it's a big decision and you need time…'

'Yes,' I said again, louder and more emphatically.

"Yes, you'll move here?'

I started to laugh and then I started to cry.

It was like a huge weight was lifted from my shoulders. I couldn't believe that Mum and I had the same idea at the same time.

The move was one of the best things I ever did.

I rented a beautiful barn conversion. The children loved it. Not only were they close to their Granny, but also my sister, their aunt, who lived next-door to the house I rented for us.

Living alongside my baby sister was wonderful. We had always gotten on well, but never really had as much time to spend together as we both would have liked. All that changed and we were in and out of each other's houses for chats and coffees and wine. I was able to spend so much more time with my mother and stepfather as well and her help with the children eased my feelings of guilt and freed me up to pursue the ultimate goal.

Work hard for five years
and be secure for life.

**Anything is possible,
you just have to be willing to take
the steps and make the changes.**

Tips for balancing family and business

Not everyone is lucky enough to have help from their family, but that doesn't mean you can't succeed.

You won't be the only one with childcare issues. Talk to your up-line, down-line and side-line. Find fellow Networkers with children and share the load. Swap babysitting duties or if there are several of you in the area use a points system. Every time you babysit you bank points, which you can then spend when you need help. My neighbour and I both worked long hours and we used to help each other out. Often she started early and I would have her children at 7am then when I worked evenings she would look after Will and Rosie. Talk to other mums, you will soon discover that you are not alone and with co-operation you can all help each other.

Check what is available in your local area. Child-minders, afterschool clubs, nursery schools are all great options. Consider taking on an Au Pair or finding a regular babysitter.

Or maybe a cleaner might offer a solution. If someone is saving you time by doing the housework then that gives you more energy and availability to spend with the family or working the business. A cleaner was my first goal, and as soon as I could afford it, I took on a gardener as well.

If you have a family, a full time job and a Network then learn to eat your lunch quickly!

Spend part of your break working on the business. As suggested above; get a cleaner and maybe a gardener as well. Buy yourself whatever free time you can.

Make sure that you involve the family in your business. Don't shut them out. The Dream Book is something for you all to share, as are the rewards and benefits you get from your growing Network. Discuss dreams, aims and goals and celebrate achievements together.

Discover the benefits of power naps.

If you find you are suffering due to long hours and lack of sleep, try and take a powernap during the day. Twenty minutes shut-eye is believed to have huge benefits to your alertness and general wellbeing.

Look after your health, but don't be afraid to work hard and put in the time. If your busy life limits the time you have available to grow your business then you may well have to put the hours in the evening or first thing in the morning. An hour spent working when the household has gone to bed can be very productive as can getting up an hour earlier than you need to.

If you really want to achieve great results then sacrifices will have to be made.

Be organised, be sensible, but not obsessive, and remember to make your family the reason for your hard work and not the excuse for failure.

I had a family rule that Friday night was kids night. I never worked and we always did something fun together, whether it was a movie night at home or sometimes we went out. No matter how busy I was, the children always had Friday evening to look forward too.

Chapter Seven

We all want to be a part of something wonderful

I don't know if it was because I now lived next door and it was so evident how well my business was growing, or if it was because her circumstance had changed, but my sister, Sam, finally decided to sign on the dotted line. It was probably a combination.

That magical timing again - You can't rush it or force it. It has to be right for each individual.

Sam had a new baby and the bridal business she was running wasn't as profitable once a full time manager had to be paid to run it for her. She saw me making money and could no longer deny the evidence before her eyes. It worked, just like Mum always said it would. You follow the plan, you put in the hours and you earn the money. No Genie or Magic Wand required here. Just time, application, hard work and a bucket load of belief.

I think Sam also saw that I was having fun. Several of my friends had joined me and the better I did the more successful they were.

Everything I learnt I passed on. Very early on I understood the basic principle of Network Marketing. It is a people business and everyone thrives with mutual help and support. I had a lot of happy friends who were all growing healthy bank balances and in control of their own working destinies. Sam didn't need to take Mum's word for it. Nor even mine, the evidence was indisputable and in her face every time my friends came round to visit.

Of course, our mother was overflowing with joy. She always knew that it was the best business in the world for us. Like offspring everywhere it took us a bit longer to reach the same conclusion.

Helping my sister get started gave me an enormous buzz.

I always enjoyed helping new starters. I loved to talk through their aims and goals and see the excitement light up on their faces when they put into words what they really want from their lives. Doing the same thing for my sister was like getting high on too much champagne. I felt so proud to be able to help her and so incredibly excited to do so.

Of course, not everyone brought into the dream. My brother, still living in South Africa, had deleted me from Facebook some time earlier in protest against the business. Now poor Sam got the same cold shoulder treatment and was also deleted.

'But he would be so good at it,' Sam said to me, pointing in annoyance at her Facebook page. 'Why is he so stubborn!'

'He's no different to you or I. Remember how mean we used to be to Mum every time she dared to mention the business?'

'I suppose…' she agreed, 'but imagine if we could get him set up over there, he would do so well and we would have a South African connection.'

I knew she was right, but I also knew that nothing we could do or say would influence him to change his mind. He had to want to join and it had to be in his own good time.

Natalie with mum and sister.

Sometime before, on a visit to the USA, I met up with an American distributor called Jan. I had met her before when she was attending a conference in UK. I found her very inspirational and knowledgeable and so I was delighted to catch up with her again. She gave me a piece of advice that was to become a large influence on my growing Network Marketing business.

'Honey, you've to get yourself a team identity,' she said

I wasn't sure what she meant and my confusion must have shown on my face.

'You've got to build a strong team identity, like a brand for you and your down-line.'

I had a background in marketing, I fully understood the importance of branding, but I wasn't
sure how I could apply it to my business –
surely the company brand was enough.

'No, Honey, I'm talking about you,' she said,
as if reading my mind. 'Go get yourself T-shirts
printed and give them to all your down-line.
Give them a shared identity.'

'T-shirts? What do I have printed on them?'

She shrugged her shoulders 'whatever you
want, Honey. Something that can give them
a shared identity. So that they become part
of something really exciting. A picture of your
head and 'Nat's Team' underneath it maybe?'

I didn't really fancy a load of Networkers all
wearing my face on their chest anymore than
I wanted 'Nat' emblazoned across everyone's
T-shirts. 'Nat's get swatted.' I said flippantly,
but I was beginning to grasp the idea she was
putting forward.

'You are going places and people will want to
go on the journey with you, Honey. You need
to create a buzz about who you are and make
everyone want to be a part of it. You need a
clear identity and a name for your network.'

I thought about it for several days. I tried to get clever, I tried to get smart, I even tried out several puns, but in the end simple wins out every time. I rang Jan.

'Got it,' I said excitedly.

'Shoot,' she replied

'I'm going to use the PowerTeam…'

'Yup, that'll do it, Honey.' She hung up.

I was a bit miffed and doubt crept in. The PowerTeam was the name from her old network and she had suggested I use it. I felt honoured and a bit overwhelmed by her generosity. Now I was wondering if she had actually meant it. Maybe I had misunderstood her. I let the doubts whirl around in my brain until the realisation finally hit me that since I had returned home, we were now in different time zones and it was still the middle of the night for her!

I waited until a more reasonable hour before I rang her back again. This time she was wide-awake and her usual friendly self. She confirmed that she was delighted for me to use her old team name.

So, I called my network, The PowerTeam, created a logo and a brand and had black T-shirts printed with a bright pink logo for the next big event we attended.

Jan was right, we created a buzz and no one could fail to recognise us.

That was only the start. She opened my eyes to the fact that everyone likes to be part of something big and successful. By creating an identity, everyone felt part of a team and pulled together to help each other. Not just because they were nice people, but to help the team grow bigger and better. Each person in my down-line wanted to contribute to the PowerTeam's growth. It was like patriotism, if I had a flag, we would all be waving it.

I loved the excitement that surrounded us.

It was like being part of a huge family. If anyone had a problem or question, there was always someone else in the group who would have help or advice to offer. I discovered that I gained as much pleasure from seeing others reach their own potential as I did from my own goal attainment. The power of Network Marketing was hard to ignore. Anyone could do well. Everyone could achieve results. Of course, that didn't mean that everyone did succeed – you still had to work hard to make it happen. But I loved the fact it was an open club and anyone could join it. I also realised that any one of my growing down-line could one day overtake me. The thought didn't send me into a competitive shiver. Instead, I found it exciting and it made me incredibly proud.

I wanted everyone in my PowerTeam to achieve everything they wanted from life and, if I could help in any tiny way then that was something to celebrate, not to fear or be challenged by.

Building and Supporting a
Team Using Facebook

Social Media has opened up a whole new world of possibilities for Network Marketing, and it can be used to recruit and to train. It is also fantastic for offering support and promoting the idea of being part of a large group of like-minded people. One of the problems new Networkers face is the fear and uncertainty that comes from not being sure about what to do or how to it.

A strong support network will keep more newbies from drifting away. They can touch base with someone at any time of day even when you, as their sponsor, are not available. There will always be someone online to see a post or comment so people never feel alone.

As well as Facebook team support, you can also set up customer focus groups for your product or service. Potential and existing customers can get involved in discussions, ask questions or simply read posts and recommendations.

Showcase your life

People buy into you. You are the person they choose to connect with, often the product/service/company are a secondary consideration. So, using your profile is very important to showcase your lifestyle and not just as a blatant advertising tool. Interesting posts will create intrigue and entice people to follow you. Eventually, curiosity may get the better of them and they will approach you wanting to know more. People will be far more open and receptive once they are aware of who you are and how you conduct your business and personal life.

Even if you have a dedicated business page, it is important to use your own photos. You need to make it personal so that people can relate to you. Use pictures to endorse your product or service, but avoid any blatant advertising. Your photos should show you building a lifestyle. Showing freedom, flexibility and luxuries. You are creating an interest in you and how you live as a result of the business choices you have made. As people are off to their nine to five job they might be looking at a new Facebook posting from you, working out at the gym or enjoying a coffee with fellow Networkers.

One of the most powerful recruiting tools is the life that you create for yourself.

A successful business gives you choice and freedom. You work hard, possibly even harder than in a conventional job. But you also work smarter and can operate around a timetable that suits your particular lifestyle. It is a powerful message and one that will resonate with other people.

It is best to have a public profile on Facebook when using it for your business. You want to be found and you want to be visible. Privacy settings will work against you.

Make sure your profile photo is of you only and not your service, products, kids or dogs

Keep your 'about info' up to date and make sure it shows what you do and that it has a link to your website.

Always be creative, positive and proactive.

Promote a team mentality

Once you have created a team identity you can encourage everyone in the down-line to be a part of it. Create team spirit by having themes at training events with your company. Not just with T-shirts, be creative. We have done everything from masks, Christmas headbands, colour dress themes to fairy wings. Aim to be the team that everyone wants to be a part of.

Everyone supports each other whether they are down-line, side-line or up-line. Remember - What you give out you get back.

Make events fun. Regardless of whether they are physical or virtual, use themes and get everyone involved. Encourage members to share pictures and posts that show the fun and co-operative side of the business.

Before, during and after team events we will recognise people for their success and achievements. Put congratulations and pat on the back posts onto their own wall as well as yours and any group/team streams. Tag anyone who you think might be interested and extend your Facebook reach with the positive energy of praising someone else. Always try to extend the tentacles of Social Networking beyond your own personal boundaries.

In the traditional job market, people rarely get praise and recognition.

In my PowerTeam, we do online business presentations through a webinar platform. I use 'GoTo webinar' but there are several other ones available. We will invite our friends, family and prospects to listen in to our key leaders as they do a presentation. It's great for helping to train new team members, but it is also a great recruiting tool. It offers an easy way to showcase the business.

For a recruiting business presentation, we produce an interesting and enticing poster with all the details on and we post it on Facebook as an invitation. The team would all share the poster on their walls and tag friends and downline into it. They would also invite people from their contact list using Facebook to the event via their personal inbox.

The aim is to spread the news of the event as far and as fast as possible. We aim to create a buzz, energy and excitement around our team and the event we are hosting.

Recruitment adverts on Facebook

It is a good idea to target these to suit the season. Use headings like - New Year - New Start - Find images (check they are free from copyright) and impose your words across them. Use your own photos of you, your family, friends and team. An image as well as words will always receives more attention. Tag potential new team members who you think might be interested and post on your personal wall occasionally and not just on your business profile.

Be attentive and observant

Facebook is about building relationships and making friends and connecting with people all around the world. Comment on and like other people posts. Show that you have a genuine interest in them. Ask questions to build up a rapport. It shouldn't be about going straight into selling your business or services. It takes time to build relationships, just like in the traditional manner of making friends.

I often initiate a conversation with someone on Facebook chat. You can see who is online and so it easy to connect. Often for me, this will be late at night when traditionally you wouldn't pick up the phone to call someone. Or some-times I send him or her a direct message, inspired by what I know their hot button is. By watching, reading and listening, I can be aware of what worries and concerns they might have. I can then offer a possible solution.

For example - I noticed you just said you didn't want to go back to work after maternity. If I could show you a way to achieve that would you have a few minutes to spare?

Assuming they say yes, I can then send a 5-minute video. Your Network will undoubtedly have something suitable. Talk to your up-line for help and advice with this, or get together with a few fellow Networkers and create your own. Personally I have several, including a video aimed at mums, one aimed more at the business, with a quick overview of our company and the types of people we are look-ing for, and my own, cartoon video of my story so far.

Some of the videos I use are just recorded from my iPhone, which I then uploaded to YouTube or Vimeo. I can then send the link to poten-tial new contacts. I also give the link to my new team members to use to help them with recruiting. I suggest they send an accompanying message with the link saying 'this is Nat, who I am working closely with. Please watch and then let me know what you find exciting.'

Follow Up Immediately

After the initial contact, assuming they agreed to watch the short video, get straight back to them with a follow up message. If they want more information either invite to a local meeting or arrange to meet them for a coffee to go through more detailed information. If they live too far away or your schedule makes a face-to-face meeting impossible, or they are just so excited that they don't want to wait another minute! Then send them a longer, more detailed overview video – your company will have something available. It might be a recorded webinar of your company's Network Plan or a video of live speakers. We made our own video and uploaded it to YouTube to use to send out as a private link for more information. More recently, we invested in recording a live business presentation with our key leaders and testimonials from lots of achievers. Your up-line will be able to help you source something suitable.

You need to get something sent out immediately. Or if you're meeting them face to face or sending them to a presentation, make sure it is within 2-3 days. Don't let their enthusiasm drain away. Modern technology means you can arrange a conversation on Skype to follow up and answer any questions, if distance creates a problem.

Whilst they are in the excited phase of wanting more info, but not yet committed, we add them to our team/prospecting group. We give them a short welcome message and ask other people to share their stories. This helps to give the 'me too' feeling. Invariably they will have questions and fears and probably been fed negatives from people outside of the business. Being in immediate touch with a network of people who have been in the same position, can be reassuring and encouraging. Hearing others say things like, 'I know how you feel. I've no experience in this either. I knew nothing about health and wellness so I felt the same. But what I found is that all the support and training is there to help you overcome it.' Will help them feel part of the team and not alone or isolated in the new business journey they are contemplating.

Often in the groups, people post their background and experience. It pays to know this information, not only because you should show an interest in the team, but also so you can buddy people up. If you are adding a teacher and you know other team members from the same profession, you can tag them to add their story.

People like to hear from others with similar backgrounds, interests and experiences. Finding business buddies along with all the positive posts and recognitions on the group Facebook feeds, will keep the right prospect intrigued. Encourage them to attend a company presentation, try to organize a meeting with you and ask them to watch planning and training videos.

Sometimes it takes a while before a potential new team member will actually sign up. The more cautiously inclined might watch and interact with the group, being drip-fed lifestyle, fun and success. Usually they do eventually decide to dive in and sign up.

Always try to seal the deal as soon as possible, but remember it isn't your job to convince. The time has to be right for them.

As soon as they do commit and sign, add them to any other team groups you have set up with a welcome message. Introduce them with a photo or a positive image and quote.

Previously, before Social Media, the excitement felt by a new member could dissipate very quickly if they were not plugged straight into a positive and supportive peer group.

Be Visible and Available

Create Facebook groups and pages so that you are available to answer questions and help your down-line no matter how far removed they are from you. This is the benefit and power of Facebook. You could have someone who lives the other end of the country or even on another continent who is in your team. They can connect to you as easily as someone who lives next door.

My Team will always see they are working directly with me. Sometimes, when posting, they will tag me in a joint message so that I can help to teach them as I respond to commonly asked questions.

Team groups work well for letting people know about trainings and events. In my PowerTeam, we run a weekly training webinar on a Sunday night. We put the link in the various team groups that it's aimed at to make sure everyone has the opportunity to tune in. We even have a team group for the leaders so that we can organise the trainings and share ideas to help each other.

It is worth keeping information in the Facebook file and photo albums for your team to use. Have a pinned post welcoming people to the page and show them how to use the group effectively, along with any other key information.

In my first planning meeting with a new team member I will show them how to access these groups and resources. I ask them to print out the pinned post as a reference to keep. Included on it is a step-by-step guide of how to get started. We also give a suggested list of what trainings to watch, websites to subscribe to and books to read.

Facebook is also great since you can screen-shot people's messages, posts and photos and use them to educate others - it adds reality when you share someone else's excited message. It might be from a new team member of some interesting company information you want to share with your team.

Facebook is a truly wonderful resource. Use it wisely and you will see your network grow and your team activity rise.

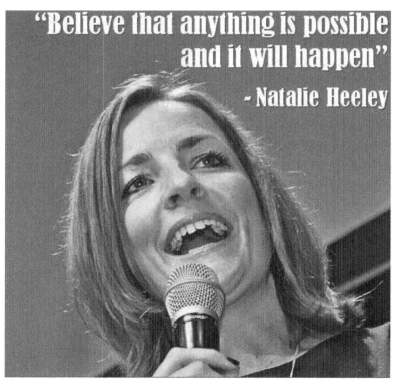

"Believe that anything is possible and it will happen"
- Natalie Heeley

Chris Munro and family

How Social Media got me involved and how it helped grow my business

By Chris Munro

Not a lot of people realise that Social Media is a very, very powerful tool and you just never know what it can do for you and how it can completely change your life!!

That's exactly what it has done for me and my family. I was using Social Media the same way as most people do, basically communicating with old school friends and old work colleagues. Also superficially connecting with people who you don't really know, probably just so that you can be nosey. Most of us use Facebook to post

pointless comments, most of them negative, boring stuff, or showing off if you've just been on holiday!

But one of those old school friends turned out to be the missing link in my life and that was none other than, Natalie Heeley.

We became friends on Facebook just like I described and that was that, no other chitter-chatter just a simple request and accept until one day Natalie could see that we had our own business which at the time was our second hair and beauty salon. She got in contact to share with us her business opportunity. But, us being ignorant, we decided that we were not interested. We didn't give Natalie the time of day to explain what the opportunity actually was!

Then we did what so many people do today and we became Facebook stalkers!

In a good way, not a creepy way. We started to notice Natalie's posts. She showcased her lifestyle. We noticed the new cars and just generally the fun and excitement that was being promoted on her Facebook page. But we still thought that we knew best and didn't contact her and still ignored her messages!

We eventually sold the hair and beauty salon and yes, you think we would have gone straight to Natalie. But no, instead, we invested £12,000 into another business. A franchise, a big mistake and even more money wasted, but that's another story. This failed enterprise did lead us back to Natalie. We watched her business and her life change and grow and we could see that she had qualified to go to Hawaii, where she was going to pick up a very nice bonus cheque!

I mean, wow, she was being flown out to Hawaii all expenses paid to pick up even more money!

This time we wanted in, the power of using Facebook correctly and effectively had worked. Natalie had made the initial invite through a Facebook message inbox, a very clever way of contacting people who you haven't spoken to for years, but without the awkwardness of calling or texting. The simple effect of showing the lifestyle of what the business was providing for Natalie and her family had worked!

This is where so many fail at Facebook and promoting their business they simply bombard their wall with advert after advert and constantly hunt people down with annoying messages. What do hunted things do? They go into hiding and before you know it nobody wants to speak to you including your best friends and family!

So we started our business in the Network Marketing world and the very first thing we did was to simply duplicate what we had learned from Natalie's approach to us and what she taught us about how to use Facebook correctly.

We copied the format and set up our own team pages on Facebook. We had one for new prospects to view and get a feel of what it was we are doing and what sort of support they would get. We would post welcomes and share everyone's success just like we had been taught to do.

We had a distributor-only page where we would also share each other's successes. This also acts as a support page where we can all gain information from each other. We post images and store files for the team to use and encourage everyone to help and motivate each other. It gives security to the team, knowing that someone will be there as and when they need that help and support which is invaluable, especially in the early days of building their businesses.

Online trainings have been key to keeping the team feel part of something special. We are all independent distributors, but to be part of a team again gives people that security. We can reach individuals from all over the country and even the World. Bringing them all together online is so important because we need to keep the same message traveling deep into the teams. We need stability and that comes from growth deep down, so it is vitally important that the message doesn't get diluted the more people join the team.

Duplication is key in Network Marketing and that is what we have all done. By working hard, keeping it simple and by duplicating a proven system has given us one of the fastest growing businesses in Natalie's group and in the UK.

Social Media can be one of your most powerful tools. But it can also destroy your business in an instance. It's all down to you and how you promote your business and mainly your life-style. It has enabled me to quit my profession and to solely work on my business. I now have a fantastic six-figure income, drive nice cars and travel all over the world. Most importantly to me, coming from a background of working away from my children, family and friends, is that I now have time.

I am free to be able to do what I want when I want as often as I want and you can't put a price on that!

Chapter Eight

Success breeds success

Life was pretty sweet; I had more money coming in than I could ever have thought possible. My team and my income were growing at an amazing rate and I was hovering around the number one spot in the UK. I don't believe it was a coincidence that my business soared once my personal life was stable and happy. Having Gladstone in my life made me a better person. I was genuinely more positive and enthusiastic, I no longer had to put a brave face on or fake a happy smile.

**Everything I had put into my
Dream Book was now my reality.**

Living near to my family was also hugely positive for me and I loved the fact that my sister was now part of the PowerTeam family.

You get back what you put out.

There was so much energy and enthusiasm surrounding me and my team that everyone wanted to be a part of it. Including, much to my surprise and delight my brother, Nick.

Before moving to South Africa he endorsed the ban on any Network Marketing conversation around the dinner table. When I finally signed up to join Mum's business he deleted me from Facebook and then Sam got the same treatment when she joined my team. He was adamant that he was never going to be a part of it.

Mum, Sam and I never spoke directly to him about the Network. But he was family and so, obviously, we talked a lot via Skype or FaceTime, text and email about our lives. He couldn't fail to see how many holidays the children and I were taking. Lifestyle will always win out when showcasing the business. Whatever negative thoughts he had about what we were doing he couldn't fail to see and be impressed by the rewards it obviously offered.

He had his own successful company in South Africa, but the business had high overheads with a big warehouse and staff. Recession had taken its toll as it had all over the world and although still getting by, order fluctuations occasionally made cash flow difficult.

'You off on holiday again?' he said, a touch of envy in his voice. 'You should come and visit us.'

'Maybe I will,' I replied, knowing that he and his family sometimes wished we were all closer to each other. I certainly understood the benefits of being near to family. Much as I loved Cape Town I was glad I didn't have to switch continents just to see Mum, Dad and Sam.

'How can you afford all the trips?'

'Well, several of them are freebies,' I said proudly, 'the company offer incentives and I keep qualifying for them.'

'Free?'

'Yes. Mum and Sam are coming on the next one with us. We are all off to Singapore next year.'

'And Mum's business pays? How? I thought she'd retired.'

I could hear the doubt in his voice and I understood. I remembered all my cynicism towards Network Marketing that had its roots in my childhood and not surprisingly he shared the same feelings. 'Well, It's not just Mum's business now. I've overtaken her on the marketing plan and even though she is more or less retired, she still qualifies for the incentives.'

'A few free flights don't really make up for loss of income though, do they? Mum must miss earning her own money.'

I was struggling to keep any hint of, 'I told you so' out of my voice. It was the first time he had shown any interest in the perks and earnings of the business and I didn't want to shut down the conversation. 'She still earns...'

'Yeah, but not like she was before.'

'No, not like before,' I agreed. 'Her income has quadrupled since she retired.'

He went quiet after that, no doubt digesting the information. I half expected a barrage of questions via email, but nothing more happened. At least not immediately. We spoke and Skyped and texted as normal and then one day the call finally came.

'Mum said you've signed Will and Rosie up for private school.' Nick said.

'I have, in fact they've already been going for a while and they love it'

'And you can really afford it?'

'Yes.'

'For both of them?'

'Yes. I would hardly do it just for one, would I?'

'But what if business drops off. Don't you worry about having to take them out next year or the year after if a new recession hits?'

'No,' I replied.

'Then you're being naive, Nat. Nothing can give you that kind of surety.'

He was part right. Nothing is certain, nothing stays the same forever and there are certainly no guarantees in life. However, no way would I gamble with my children's education. 'I don't worry about the fees, Nick, because I have them covered.'

'Yes, for a term, or maybe a year...'

'No,' I said, interrupting him. 'I have them covered.'

'For how long?' he asked quietly, finally beginning to get just how powerful the business was.

'For as long as it takes.'

'Ok,' he said, following a long pause, 'tell me what I have to do.'

My brother got started just like everyone else. The fact that he was thousands of miles away, simply meant we had to work initially without connecting physically. We did everything online, starting with his planning meeting. He wrote his contact list, I sent him trainings and made him sit down with the family to fill out the dream book together.

Nick gave me a couple of his friend's details he thought might be interested in joining him. I sent our business presentation to them and added them to our Facebook group. I followed up with a conversation via Skype and very quickly Nick had his first team members registered.

It was all very exciting.

Nothing beats the thrill of helping people close to me set out on a journey of achievement. I wanted to do more to help and decided it was time I paid South Africa a visit. Not only would I see Nick, my lovely sister-in-law and my nephew, but I could also expand the business into a brand new International direction.

I booked myself a business class ticket. A luxury that my accountant assured me was a tax-deductible item and prepared for my trip.

Between us, Nick and I organised a couple of business presentations for me to do while I was in Cape Town.

I sent out Facebook messages saying I was off to South Africa and invited anyone with contacts out there to join me at the business presentations. My Network shared the message and as a result I was able to meet up with and recruit a few additional new team members during my visit.

The trip wasn't all work

I took the opportunity to visit one of my favourite places. An hour's drive from Cape Town, some say that Cape Point is the most southerly point in South Africa. The spot where, many believe, the Indian and the Atlantic Oceans meet. Visitors flock to witness the two seas splashing together, they marvel at the spectacular cliffs, visit the lighthouse and browse in the curio shops.

When my Dad settled for a while in South Africa his first home wasn't far from there, at a place called Simons Town. I often visited Cape Point with my father, so the place is full of lovely memories as well as being a beautiful national park.

It was a lovely, clear, sunny morning and Nick, his wife and their son Josh decided to join me. The scenery was as breathtakingly lovely as I remembered it being. But Josh was more interested in finding the monkeys that roam the area than he was in admiring the view.

'Where are they all?' he asked, staring out of the window as though wishing alone would make them appear.

We parked the car and walked to the edge of the continent. The farthest south you can go without tipping into the sea.

We were so lucky with the weather because, on a clear day, the views are breathtaking. We settled down for a picnic lunch followed by a short stroll along the coastline. I loved every second and soaked up the wonderful images to take home with me. I knew that next time I saw Dad he would want to hear all about it.

Only Josh was disappointed by the visit. Not a monkey to be seen.

We headed back towards the car, relaxed and chatting, while Josh ran ahead. I felt incredibly fortunate to be able to spend such quality time with my brother and his family and wished we all lived closer. At least the business, with its generous travel perks, would allow us to all see more of each other.

An excited yelp from Josh made us hurry towards the car park. Our car was alive with monkeys. They covered every possible surface.

'Look,' I said, pointing to the front of the car, where a large male monkey sat proudly watching as a mother and her babies ran across the bonnet.

Josh was delighted, his Dad not so much. Monkeys have been known to cause damage to paintwork and can be difficult to remove from cars. Nick shouted and waved his arms around, but the family and their accompanying friends seemed unmoved and determined to stay where they were.

Josh pulled an uneaten sandwich from the picnic bag and moved closer so they could get the scent. It was enough to capture their interest, but they still showed no inclination to move.

Nick looked at his watch, 'we've got to get going soon,' he said.

I nodded in agreement. We had a meeting booked early that evening with a couple of potential new team members.

The car alongside us drove away, exposing a family that had been out of view, enjoying a picnic of their own. Suddenly the large male monkey leapt from the car and charged towards the family. The entire troop followed after him.

We took the chance to quickly get into the car and start the engine. As we drove away we saw all the monkeys hurrying away with stolen sandwiches.

It was wonderful to combine a business trip with the very real pleasure of seeing my brother and his family again. I experienced the same thrill that helping Sam to get her business going had given me. It really was a family affair now and I knew how pleased and proud Mum was with us all.

'You never know,' Nick said, with a smile, as I was preparing to leave, 'I might end up over-taking you in the business plan.'

I hugged and kissed him and said goodbye. 'Wow, that would be fantastic.' I replied.

What other industry could turn competition into enhanced success? If Nick or any of my down-line overtook me then I would be delighted. I was never in it for the glory of being the best. It was always about lifestyle and security for myself and my children. The better everyone else did, the more money I would earn. I was already scaling down on the time I put into my business. A few more years and I could be like my mother – earning more and more each year for doing less and less.

Natalie taking on the world...

Tips on going International

Working at a distance is pretty much the same as working the domestic market. However, it helps if your overseas recruits have a bit of confidence since you can't physically be there to help and encourage them.

You have to be prepared to put in the Skype time even if being in a different time zone makes it inconvenient. They need to be self-starters and motivated, but will still require face-time with you.

Make sure they have access to all the online trainings and resources. You risk losing them if they struggle to access information and training. I have recorded many webinars and uploaded them to platforms like YouTube or Vimeo so that teams can access them at any time of day - all of my leaders share their own too so we have a library of recordings that the team can use.

Together
Everyone
Achieves
More

Social Networking really makes building overseas business a realistic possibility. Make sure you include them in groups and postings, make them feel a part of your team. Then once they have enough members they can set up a new group for that country and build their own team spirit.

Help them to make contact with other Networkers from your company living in the area. Find out about meetings, trainings and conferences running in that country. Mixing with others will help to keep them motivated. Try to buddy people up.

Encourage them to expand and build their own team as quickly as possible. Feeling part of something rather than working in isolation makes everything so much easier and more worthwhile.

Get them to make a list of any contacts in your country so that you can help them build a team here as well as at home. Work with them and any down-line they have.

Use your contacts and Network to help them grow their business. Ask your up-line, down-line and even side-line if anyone has friends or contacts in that country that might like to hear about the business opportunity.

Once you have a few people in the new team, set up a weekly or bi weekly online meeting with them - it always helps if you can all see each other platforms like Google Hangout, Fuze, or Go To meeting, are all great for this.

Overseas business building can be deducted from tax. Check with your accountant for details about what is allowable.

Chapter Nine

Don't just work hard – work smart

A hundred years ago, horses still pulled carts and cars were considered a strange, new, fancy gimmick for the rich and privileged. The telephone was replacing the telegraph and photos were black and white, or more accurately a strange sepia colour. Man had only just managed his first, faltering flight, let alone landed on the moon. Technology, the speed and supply of information and the ability to communicate with the world were all the stuff of science fiction.

Change is inevitable. You cannot expect to thrive in a modern, highly connected world if you can't accept this. If you want to be in business today you need to understand how Social Networking works. You might choose not to embrace all of it, but ignore the opportunities it offers and your drive for success will suffer. This is especially true if you have been in Network Marketing for ten years or more. The old way of building Multi-Level businesses is far slower than embracing technology and all it has to offer. When I started within our company I was thirty and I was one of the youngest. I was part of a small minority, but now the tables have turned. The industry is getting younger and younger as people embrace Social Media and use it to Network.

Social Networking undoubtedly has its flaws and its limitations, but on the flip side it opens up the world from your desktop, Smartphone or tablet. You have immediate access to people across the globe. If you are shy or unsure then the social media platforms will give you the chance to build your business with limited physical interaction, allowing your confidence to grow. Soon you'll find you can approach anyone in person.

I have seen my business grow at an astonishing rate and I know that a huge part of my success is due to my embracing the brave new world of Social Media. Throughout this book I have suggested how to use Facebook effectively. I wasn't an avid Facebook user when I started out. I am self-taught, learning as I went along through trial and error. I now have a system set up for team members to use and duplicate. I started from scratch and learnt from many in my team. I also enlisted some outside help for team trainings.

Don't be a dinosaur – embrace change.

I won't repeat everything previously covered so the section on Facebook is limited in this Chapter to a short piece on training. But there are plenty of other avenues to look at and I have enlisted the help of a couple of my down-line who use Twitter and other platforms to great effect. Both Beth and Laila are hugely successful and highly experienced in Network Marketing

Facebook for training your team

Facebook team groups have become the primary method for training the team, creating an online community of like-minded people. It keeps everyone constantly connected, so they don't have to feel alone or isolated. A new business venture can feel overwhelming and daunting if you don't have suitable support.

Files can be used for sharing team documents. You can upload links for training videos, which we record on YouTube or Vimeo and then use the link - this might be a training webinar from a system like GoTo Webinar, that is then uploaded onto YouTube, or just posting a direct video from your company of you sharing a message with your team via your Smartphone.

This facility to use a pinned post to highlight the most important information and training videos, as well as a How-To guide for your team is incredible. Beware though, that if people are on their phone or tablet they need to actually click on the pinned post, so show them in your planning meetings, whereas on a desktop it is clearly visible.

Being able to constantly recognise your team members by tagging them in a post and sharing a photo or a motivational image. People love to see their name in lights, no matter how big or small, it empowers people quickly and helps to build their confidence and allows them to feel special in front of the peers.

Use it to promote upcoming trainings or a live webinar by tagging the team or tagging the leaders to tag their team.

We use it to create themes. When we are at a company event we will promote that the whole team is dressing in a certain colour, so that we have a unique team profile and energy - people love feeling part of something special.

You can use it to recommend your products or services by product placement, seasonal promotions and other networking stories.

I suggest you have customer support groups as well as team and training groups.

Using Twitter

Beth Mansfield has built a successful Network using Social Media, especially Facebook and Twitter. She teaches her down-line how to use these mediums effectively, and sometimes her up-line as well!

If you don't know how to do something then ask – that's what the team is there for.

My name is Beth Mansfield and I'm 25 years old and have been involved with Network Marketing for three years.

Before I came across Multi-Level Marketing, I was a single mum and worked in retail, the hours were long and the pay was awful. So I started up two small businesses.

Being a single mum to my little boy who was under two at the time, I often felt that I needed to duplicate myself just to get through the week. Being self-employed was great, but I had no work/life balance. I was missing out on the precious moments of my little boy growing up.

Everything has changed since I joined a Network Marketing company. I am able to spend so much time with him now doing things that we both love. My son is now six and this year, thanks to MLM I am able to pay for his full private school tuition on my independent income.

Being able to provide the lifestyle I want for my son is incredible.

MLM has given me the freedom to dream again, to become the person I have always wanted to be, but most importantly to show thousands of other their potential to do incredible things.

For me, it's not a job it's a passion.

My Top Tips for Twitter

Find your USP – you need to identify what is your unique selling point. For example - fitness freak, horse lover, traveller.

You need to be interesting and to stand out from the crowd. That means truly identifying who you are and what your strengths are and then finding the right audience to connect with and to market to.

Don't try and be someone or something that you are not. People will see straight through it ... BE YOU, only better... No one else can play that role as well as you can.

Be passionate - once you have found your USP, develop it, promote it and be proud. No one will follow someone who is unsure or uncommitted.

Think about your first statement or title on Twitter. It needs to be eye-catching and bold. It needs to be straight to the point and with great key words that capture people's attention.

Make your Twitter account interesting and something people will want to follow? Be honest and ask yourself - would you really want to follow you?

Have a professional profile but don't be a bore. Your profile photo needs to be professional, but fun. People don't want to see a selfie with you and your best friend drinking Tequila in Turkey. Keep that for Instagram or Pinterest. Your Twitter account should portray everything that you represent. Who you are and who you want to be. You need to create a web presence worth following. Your photo and profile are like a shop window, they need to be interesting, intriguing and enticing.

Be eye-catching but always professional. Be aware - you never know who is watching.

Simple is best - Keep your @ name simple - people like simple. And if you can keep all of your social media platform names the same
@example
example@facebook
Instagram.example
Etc.

It helps people to find you. After all, that is the point - we all want to be found.

Interact - Twitter is all about networking, so network. Find people whose interests are similar to yours, who enjoy the same things, and people that you would like to connect with.

You literally have the whole world at your fingertips. That's a powerful thought, so use it.

Search hot topics that are trending as well the people who are interested in similar things to you.

Favourite other people's posts. It shows that you have common ground and that you are interacting. It will bring your profile to people's attention.

Retweet any relevant or interesting information. You will attract like-minded people.

Quantity is good in business but quality is always better.

Twitter is full of hidden gems; you just need to spend a bit of time finding them.

Keep Tweets short and sweet. Creativity needs constraints and simplicity is at our core. Tweets are limited to 140 characters so they can be consumed easily anywhere, even via mobile text messages. There's no magical length for a Tweet, but a recent report by Buddy Media revealed that Tweets shorter than 100 characters get a 17% higher engagement rate.

Tweet often. There is no rule of thumb for how many times you can tweet in a day, but the general rule is you can tweet when you want, that's the joy of Twitter.

However, I personally stick to 4 or 5 tweets a day. Find what time your audience is online and actively interacting. It is trial and error, but you will soon learn when your posts receive the most attention.

So, happy Tweeting and hope that my top tips help.

Using Twitter – Thoughts by Laila Ali

I am thirty years old and live in Birmingham, England. Previously I have worked in many jobs from Hairdresser to Employment and Support work. I've always loved helping people and that is what Network Marketing is all about. I only began this journey in February 2013 and already it has completely transformed my life. I can now cope with rejection, face my personal fears and deal with difficult situations. I have changed as a person and I am now confortable in my own skin. Most importantly of all I am able to give my sister, Sami, a better life and know that her future is secure.

It takes time and patience to build a following on Twitter. Don't be tempted to buy followers, it just looks desperate and is nearly always obvious. Be open, honest and passionate and you will gradually build a band of loyal followers.

Make sure that you have an engaging profile and photo and be active by posting at least once a day. Take the time to pre-plan, especially if you are busy. Know what you want to say in advance and think carefully about what to post. I recommend no more than 20% should be business related. Use all social media to showcase your lifestyle and your interests. Be aware of the people you are connected with. What do they like? What do you have in common? Demonstrate your personality and your lifestyle on Twitter. Be transparent and always friendly. Then, if people connect with you it will be because they can relate to you and find you interesting.

Recruiting posts are boring and ineffective. Instead, tweet about what you do and how you help people. Let your passion, positivity and enthusiasm shine through.

Be aware of what's happening on Twitter. What are the people you follow posting? Interact with at least twenty-five people every day. Show that you are interested and can be bothered to engage with other tweeters.

You can use your Twitter account to link to other platforms by ticking the box in your settings, but always check that a post is appropriate and will still work in another medium. It can appear lazy if you simply cross-post everything. Sometimes, the perfect comment in Twitter makes no sense at all if posted onto Facebook.

Learn how to use the hashtag effectively. You can look for what people are saying by using Hashtag (#) via search. Use an App called Tags for Likes too, this can be great and very effective for other platforms such as Instagram. Use the information to tap into the buzz and create excitement around your own posts.

Attach your own images to quotes and inspirational thoughts. If linked to Facebook it will all merge automatically.

Instagram

Thoughts on using Instagram
by **Beth Mansfield**

Instagram is great fun and everyone should have it. Images are a great FREE way to advertise your lifestyle, product or service via Instagram.

Hundreds of thousands of people use Instagram on a worldwide basis daily, so tapping into this market is great and will help your business grow from strength to strength.

Instagram allows you to post short videos as well as pictures, which can be an effective tool for your business.

Like many social media platforms the principles always stay the same - maintain your USP at all times no matter which social media site you use. Keep it easy to remember and up to date with current and interesting events.

Know what your network of people are interested in. Once you learn and understand that fact, you will be able to attract a wider audience. More likes equals more views. More hits or views, means you will generate more traffic. The more people who look at your content the more successful you will be.

So, what are my top tips for Instagram and how do I recruit from there?

Balance fun images with pictures from your business - Instagram is not just an opportunity for your business. It is a place where you can have fun and project your lifestyle, interests and personality into your profile. It keeps it interesting - use the 80/20 rule here too. 80% you 20% business

Cultivate a following - Connect your Instagram with your Facebook and Twitter accounts, but keep track of your postings as not everything makes sense on other platforms.

Use relevant, popular hashtags

Engage by following others and liking their photos - the more you interact with other people the more traffic you will direct to your page.

Cross-post selected images to your Facebook page with a hashtag that aligns with your campaign or brand image to help people who don't already know that you are on Instagram to find you.

Use hashtags that are trending and relevant #business #money #freedom #recruiting #health #beauty #fun #followback

Follow your Followers Back - The people you follow on social networking platforms make all the difference in the world. Curiously, many brands on Instagram (some with very large followings) don't follow back.

To create strategic friendships on Instagram, find the people you enjoy interacting with and can learn from. Follow them or follow them back.

**You don't have to be great to start,
but you do have to start to be great.**

Really, play around with filters and different techniques that Instagram allows you to use. Take the time to learn the medium and be creative. The saying is true - A great picture really can say a thousand words.

Engage with other Instagram users. Like other people's photos and leave positive comments for them to read. Follow your already established followers from other social media platforms.

Always Include your hashtags - if your brand uses specific hashtags on Twitter or Google+, use them on Instagram as well.

Promote the company photos – They are free marketing tools.

Have Fun! Instagram is all about showing people who you are and promoting all of the great things happening in your life thanks to Multi-level marketing.

Top tip from Laila Ali

When you have a really good picture/post on Facebook take a screenshot and put it on Instagram. Make sure it is something interesting and intriguing that will capture people's imagination or jump-start their curiosity. Then direct them back to the full post on Facebook or to your website for more details.

Pinterest

Notes from Laila Ali

Pinterest is like your dream book or dream board in a virtual world for everyone to see.

You can create personal mood boards and goal boards to highlight and promote your lifestyle, interests and dreams. Do it well and they can attract interest and inspire others to follow you and maybe even to join you on your adventure.

It is very easy to set up an account with Pinterest – just follow the instructions, they are self-explanatory. When you reach the section in your settings regarding other social media, you can choose to tick the boxes to inter-link all of your activities.

You can have more than one Pin board and it makes sense to keep your interests separate and therefore focused. It makes it easier for people to understand what you are about and will help to grow your follower base. For instance, you could have one for business and one for travel. The two are actually linked since the business activities are what fund the travel.

Initially, you may attract interest from others who are interested in travelling and if you maintain their attention and they become a follower and eventually they may look at your other activities and jump across to other social media platforms that you are on.

By making sure that everything is interlinked it makes it easier for cross-platform exploration by your followers.

You need to be active and try to pin something new two or three days a week. If you go silent for too long then your number of followers drops away.

Take the time to explore Pinterest. You will find boards on almost every subject. Follow lots of other people and share their posts.

The principle of Pinterest is simple

Find – Learn – Share – Follow

Linkedin

Notes from Laila Ali

LinkedIn is not the same as the other social media platforms and needs to be treated in a different way. It is aimed at the jobs market, designed to help professionals interact and connect. You need to regard it in that context. Make sure that your profile picture is clear and slightly more serious. No fun or silly poses on LinkedIn.

Make sure that your personal profile is up-to-date and makes it clear why you are on there – you want to connect with like-minded individuals who are keen to build a business and be successful.

Make sure you list all the skills that are relevant to you and your business.

Pay attention to spelling and grammar. Punctuation might not matter on Facebook or Twitter, but it gets noticed if it is wrong on LinkedIn.

Try to connect with people who might be relevant to whatever network business you operate in. You might be interested in sales people or with marketing backgrounds, the self-employed or those who already have their own companies. Or if your network business is with nutrition or health then target individuals already in the industry. Just try to connect with as many relevant professionals as possible.

Be interactive and helpful. If someone posts that they are looking for a new employee, pass the information on if you think it might be relevant to someone else you are connected with. A favour can often be repaid to your advantage at a later time. Think of it like attending a regular networking meeting where you would talk and help each other out.

Contact and connect with anyone you have worked with in past employment. Who knows what they are doing now, they might be looking for exactly the opportunity your business is offering. Simply by making the connection could lead to a new team member.

Post updates and success stories.

Message people personally to build relationships.

Connect with networks and be part of the LinkedIn community.

When you post anything, include an image whenever you can. A visual stimulant always attracts more attention.

Give endorsements and thank anyone who endorses you.

Ask for recommendations from your connections and display any written testimonials.

You can join any existing relevant groups or even start your own to help you build relationships.

Laila Ali- Top Tips and facts regarding Social Media in general.

90% of her new business comes through social media.

She works on the basis that her audience will not only be on one platform so she operates on all of them so that she can interact with every potential new team member possible.

Allow people to see who you really are. They want to know who it is they are dealing with. Let your personality shine through.

Understand that people don't only look for

what you post, but are looking for what you don't post! In other words, they are trying to build a profile on who and what you really are. So be transparent and open.

Don't lose your unique identity. Stay true to you.

Be wary of buying fake likes and followers. Although it gives the appearance that you have appealed to thousands and that can bring in more followers, fake likers are usually easy to spot and are a turnoff for other, more genuine followers.

If you set up a selling page on any outlet, keep it focused and brief. Use a great image and make sure the words are clear and focused. Create interest and link to a business page or website for further details.

Tagging is a fantastic tool. If you tag someone in a Facebook post then that goes out to their friends as well. But use it sparingly, don't be a nuisance. When Lalla accepts a new friend request from a new team member she always sends out a welcome message, tagging them into it. Often it creates interest from their friends, wanting to know more about what they are up to.

Final word on social media

It is important to check when posting pictures or even words, that what you are saying is compliant with your company's rules. Be careful about making claims. If in any doubt check with your network marketing company first. They all have compliance rules. Beware how quickly things can go viral. Great when you have something wonderful to say, show and promote. Not so good when it is against good practice or regulations.

Remember as well that Social Networking is about making friends wherever you go and whenever you can. It takes time to build up relationships with people and even longer online than it would be in person.

You can use Social Media as a follow-up for when you have physically met someone. Use it as an extension to your face-to-face networking.

Chris Munro and my sister joined me after years of seeing my posts - I have dozens of others that have done the same, some of which are from a completely cold market like, Gemma Easdon, and Beth Turner who are now one of my fastest growing teams.

You are putting the time in now and sowing the seeds to reap your harvest in months and years to come.

As one of my favourite networkers, Jim Rohn, would say 'everyone must choose one of two pains: the pain of discipline or the pain of regret' so be consistent.

Managing time is always a challenge, so I would recommend that you choose two or three platforms and concentrate on doing them really well. If you are very busy and struggle to maintain the constant activity required for effective social media management, then look at using a scheduling tool like Hootsuite or Buffer. You can set them up to deliver content at pre-set times on your behalf.

If you want to build a massive business in Network Marketing then get online now and master the skills of Social Media.

Chapter Ten

Money Matters

It has been an incredible journey for me. Ten years ago, if I had walked into a fortune-teller's tent and they had told where I would be and what I would have achieved today I would have condemned them as a charlatan.

I honestly never, ever believed that I would join the world of Multi- Level marketing. I certainly couldn't envisage how it would transform my life and that of my family, or that I could ever earn so much money and enjoy such an exciting lifestyle.

Eight years ago, when I finally signed on the dotted line I thought the business would give me a little bit extra every month. Now I earn more in a month than most people earn in a year.

As I've said throughout this book, I'm not endowed with special gifts or insights. I truly believe that anyone can replicate what I have done. That is the wonder of the business model. You certainly don't need to be a superstar sales person or have a degree or be a math wizard. All you need to do is learn from your up-line, side-line, down-line and work hard. With Social Media so easy to use you can build a network and be earning money so much faster than I ever managed to achieve.

For two years I played at the business and earned a few hundred pounds a month. When I finally started to take it seriously it grew rapidly into a decent income and a couple of years after that I began to earn serious money.

In October 2011 my Bonus cheque for the month was £3051.30

In October 2012 my Bonus cheque for the month was £4690.80

I quote the figures above because this is the kind of income I think most people work hard to aspire to earn. Way above the national average, but not so high that it goes into impossible dream territory.

My monthly Bonus for October 2013 was considerably more than double what it was for the same period 2012 and 2014 was unbelievably high. So much so that I am not going to quote it, as I'm not here to impress you, but to impress upon you just what is possible. I will tell you that one month's bonus for this year is more money than most people aspire to earn in a year.

Figures published by the Office for National Statistics state that in the year to April 2012 the average annual salary for full-time workers in the UK was £26,500.

My earnings now are beyond anything I could ever have imagined possible.

Below is my yearly volume that gives some indication of the incredible growth that has taken place in my business, which I like to call the snowball effect. For those of you who are unfamiliar with Multi-Level Marketing, every company has a way of tracking your business activity, which I will call, units. Whether it is through sales of products or services or through recruiting and training new team members. You also earn units based on your team activity and so, the larger and more active your team, the more volume that is credited to you. Your earnings are based on that volume. Which is why training and support are so important. You succeed more when your team succeeds more.

In 2010 my volume of units awarded for the year was 1773

In 2011 my volume of units awarded for the year was 1771

In 2012 my volume of units awarded for the year was 2439

In 2013 my volume of units awarded for the year was 5700

In 2014 my volume of units awarded for the year (so far) is 12500

In monetary terms already this year my volume turnover is just short of £9 million in the UK alone! By year-end I will have passed that magical ten million mark. I More than doubled my volume from the year before.

It gives you an indication of how application and hard work pay off. This is the compound result of working my business every day and the exponential growth that resulted from it.

When you start out you put way more hours in than you get paid for. But work it well and eventually you get paid for way more hours than you actually work.

The growth that I have experienced in the last 3 years is down to the work I started doing 6 years ago. I continued to work consistently every single day and set up systems that were easy to duplicate, expanding and adapting for social media use on those best practices that my amazing leaders John and Jayne have developed over the last 20 years.

But I never imagined it would snowball so much, surpassing my expectations way beyond my Dream Book goals.

Committing to send the kids to private school two years ago was the turning point for me. Having made the decision, I was petrified of letting them down. So I worked and worked, and kept on working, even when the money really started to pile up. I wanted and needed to know they were totally secure. Not just for one year, but for all the years to come. Then onwards to University should they wish to. At the moment Will wants to be a pilot and Rosie is planning on being a vet. That means a lot of years to come with me supporting them and paying fees. I want them to leave their education totally debt free. As I see it, that is the best thing that I, as a parent, can do for them. It will set them up for whatever their chosen future might be.

**My children have always
been what motivate me.
They are the wind beneath my wings.**

Now, we not only have financial security, but we all have an amazing lifestyle. This year I have taken twelve holidays, ten of them involving flights. As a family, we aim to go away every school break and we all have a say in choosing the destination.

During the past year I have worked less hours. But my business has still more than doubled. In an average week I probably work no more than twenty-five – thirty hours now.

Over the past two months it has been considerably less than that. I've had to take time off due to a back problem. Between enforced bed rest and almost daily treatments, my business has had to tick along without me. I feel privileged that my down-line, my up-line and on occasions even my side-line have all stepped up to help. Not that the business has needed much in the way of support. It now runs like a perfectly tuned and well-oiled machine and the money keeps on coming in, but I never like to let my new team members down.

I have been able to pay for private healthcare without having to worry about or even question how much it will cost me.

I have to pinch myself occasionally to make sure that I am alive and that it's all real. I never take my good fortune for granted. But I don't play down or belittle my achievements either.

Dave O'Connor has always taught me to have 'an attitude of gratitude'.

I had help and support and for that I am so thankful. Now it is my turn to pass it on and pay it forward.

The Infrastructure of trainings and online prospecting tools I have set up with my leaders over the past 3-4 years has meant people are achieving their goals faster than ever. As a result, someone is smashing every new record previously set.

For me, a real measure of my success is for my team to break my records. I can't wait to celebrate the first team member who overtakes me on the marketing plan. I will know I have laid the path to success for all of my down-line. As Gemma Easden, in my team calls it, we have laid the perfect yellow brick road to help people achieve their dreams. It is incredibly satisfying to see others achieving their dreams and knowing that I have helped in some way.

We all have the same hours in the day. But our team members are blessed with amazing tools that have taken years of experience from my leaders to set up, but now, any new networkers can run with them.
Most have no idea how easy it is now compared to when we started. I would say and stress that Multi-Level Marketing works best when everyone helps and supports each other.

My rise through the marketing plan started very slowly. By comparison I have seen new starters fly. Everyone is different and I have learnt that each team member has his or her own journey to make. I have no right to put any limitations or expectations onto them by comparing how long it took me. We all set out with different qualities and different challenges. Some people start at incredible speed, others drift for a while and then, when they are ready, they suddenly find their feet and run with it. Never give up on a slow, new starter. What I love is that every new dawn gives us the chance to draw a line in the sand and start again. I don't suppose my up-line (not even my

Mum) saw anything in me, during my first two years in the business that gave any hint of the incredible future I was about to embrace.

Being a leader, developing a team means thinking of others more than you. If you help enough networkers to get what they want from the business, you will get more than you ever desired. This is a really worthwhile life lesson and one that I have passed on to my children.

Aside from the financial and lifestyle benefits that my business has given to us all, I honestly feel that we are better people.

My kids are so thoughtful - every teacher comments on how well they treat and care for others. They are kind and considerate. They always try to do their best. I teach them that they can have anything in life, as long as they have the belief and they can see themselves achieving it and be willing to put the necessary effort in. I will believe in them until the day that they can fully understand and appreciate that truth for themselves. Believing that they can and will achieve anything they want from life.

I tell them to always be positive and I have tried to instill strong self-worth and confidence. They have accompanied me onto the stage and spoken on several occasions and stood in front of hundreds and at times even thousands of people. They understand and already value a strong work ethic. Despite them being so young, they know what it has taken me to deliver their lifestyle. That is because they have been a part of the journey with me, right from the beginning with that very first entry into the Dream Book to take them to Disney.

My children always push me to aim for next level. As soon as I reach a promotion they look at the marketing plan with me.

'Mummy, when will we do that level?' Will or Rosie will say.

They always say 'we' because that's how it has always been. We are in it together, as a family. Although it has never been my goal to try to reach a certain position or get the biggest cheque. The children do stretch me, when they see what others are achieving it makes me want to show them what's possible. They give me the reason to keep moving forward. They could present the business in their sleep, as it is so much an integrated part of our lives.

Our Dream Book has taught my children to have big dreams and big ambitions and to know that everything is possible.

The most wonderful feeling for me is that I know they are proud of their mummy. One of my driving forces is for them to say in their adult years, 'wow mummy, you did all that for us.'

They know that we are a solid unit and we have freedom of choice and financial security.

My plan for the future is to slow down and enjoy life. To have the luxury of time - to continue to be there for everything with the kids, and to enjoy a great future with my partner. I will continue to support my wonderful PowerTeam, which now has over 2500 people placing orders each month just in the UK. That's without my growing global business. Many Networkers track their business on how many distributors they have in total, but for me that is not a true measure. For me, it is about how many are active and that means placing orders and recruiting and training new team members. I want to see all of them fly high up the promotion ladder and achieve more than they ever thought possible. I would love for all of them to achieve as much or even more than I have.

I want all of my successful team to pay it forward.

To know I have helped one person fills me with pride, but to help thousands in some way is incredible.

Always remember to be true to yourself. Arrogance and ego has no place on any company's marketing plan. Be gracious and generous and willing to give out help, support and advice.

I started this business to be there for my children and I will always be true to myself - the hard work is done and now the future begins.

As John Curtis told me, 'you can work five years hard and then never have to work again.'

I don't know if I truly believed him at the time, but I certainly know it to be true now.

Network Marketing offers an incredible opportunity to anyone prepared to embrace it.

Put traditional methods of MLM and Social Media together and work smart and hard and it is like releasing the handbrake on your business.

As I approach the end of the book I am going to give you a few simple facts and figures from Bob Parker, who has spent 20 years in the Network Marketing industry and is also the Vice Chairman of the UK DSA (Direct Selling Association)

The MLM industry in the UK is worth about £2 billion.

There are around 450,000 active distributor/ agents.

75% of them are female.

80% of them are part-time. However, this percentage figure is decreasing. More people are going full time each year.

Across Europe there are around 12 million distributors/ agents with a turnover of over £20 billion.

The trends across the DSA in the UK show an increase in the over 50's getting involved.

It also shows an increase in the under 30's. Particularly, in the young mum's sector.

A few final tips for when it all goes well…
Holidays and sports cars are fun and we all need rewarding for our hard work and success. But remember why you started the journey and stay true to the goals in your Dream Book.

When the money starts coming in, get sound financial advice. Don't take on huge financial commitments as soon as you start making big money - you need to have a solid structure and that takes time to cement. You will need an accountant as a self- employed person and at some stage he\she will probably recommend you set up a limited company to best manage your income.

A good accountant will be able to advise you about tax and allowable expenses.

Learn to manage your time effectively and don't ever forget or exclude your family – make them the reason and not the price for your success. You never want to look back and see you missed out on time with your family - so have a balance from day one.

You can buy yourself extra time by bringing in help. As previously suggested, a cleaner and a gardener can help enormously. But also, as your team grows, you might benefit from employing some administration help or even a Personal Assistant.

And finally…

I truly believe that if you follow your dreams, back them up with goals and hard work you can achieve whatever you want. Believe in yourself and what you do and the right people will come into your life.

My friend and mind mentor, Dave O'Connor, told me that I needed a new challenge. I decided to write a book and started to make some notes. I knew I would need some help, but had no idea how to find a writer to accompany me through the process.

Then an old school friend joined the business and through her I met one of her contacts whose mother was a writer named Linda Dunscombe.

Be positive and positive people will come into your life. If you ask the Universe correctly, it never fails to deliver.

I know my children and grandchildren have a legacy for life and that makes me very proud. My amazing Mum is enjoying her retirement and in the three years since she retired her income has more that quadrupled. That is the power of Network Marketing.

I'll be eternally grateful to my family, Mum, Dad, my Step-Dad Peter, my brother Nick and my sister Sam and of course my 'why' Will and Rosie and my close friends, Jen, Rach, Louise, Claire, Hannah, Sharon, Vanda, my Gran and Gladstone who have supported me and believed in me. They have been there through the tough times and the good times and there have been plenty of both. Some have joined me, some still might. For some the time may never come, but they've never judged me and I know they are all so proud of me.

And to all my mentors, particularly John Curtis and Jayne Leach, Jan Ruhe and my incredible mindset guru Dave O'Connor, my company for providing an unshakeable plan and for having incredible vision. Also, all the distributors in my side-line who have given me their time and encouragement, for which I am truly grateful. My leaders, who are too many to name, but they know who they are and of course my team who inspire me daily.

TEAM = Together, Everyone Achieves More!

Thank you for reading my story, I hope it helps you to achieve your own goals and to realise your own dreams.

I wish you ongoing success.

Natalie x

Acknowledgements

Just ten months ago I had a dream to write a book, primarily to help people just like me to have the belief and courage to embark on a journey in the Network Marketing industry. Although as a child I dreamt of being a journalist my writing skills didn't develop as much as I would have liked. Like building a network, you cannot do it alone and the production of this book has been made possible only by using a team of people. Together we have made my dream a reality.

One of the first rules I learnt in the industry is to recognise other people so much that you do not need any recognition for yourself.

Thank you to my Mum, Jan Whittaker, for being my rock through the many struggles and challenges I have had over the years - you never stopped believing me and you were, and are, the biggest support to me as a single Mum. For Will and Rosie, you are the best Granny they could ever ask for.

I've met some inspirational people throughout my journey. My mentors, John Curtis and Jayne Leach - thank your for pioneering such systems for us to duplicate and for seeing a little of bit of yourselves in me. You took me under your wings and gave me the belief and courage to fly.

Jan Ruhe, you have taught me so much about team spirit. We've had so many late night conversations over Facebook and I am forever grateful that you encouraged me to launch my PowerTeam.

To my dear friend, Dave O'Connor, who has programmed my mind and taught me to get through every challenge thrown down on my journey and he still continues to push my goals and dreams to places I never imagined possible.

To my best friend and partner, Gladstone Small. It is no wonder my business has flown in the last two years - happiness is a great place to be.

To Julianna Woods, for being always by my side when the going gets tough and always there to celebrate our journey together.

To my old neighbour, Hannah Wylde, who has never understood how much she has supported me with the kids when I was living so far away from my family. Also, to my baby-sitter, Bethany Mullaly.

To Sander Jurkiewicz, my photographer, who has got an eye for capturing the moment like nobody else.

Chris Petitjean, for believing in me in my early days and showing me that you don't have to do what others perceive as 'normal' to be successful - he showed me that it was Ok take a risk, and he gave me the courage to do so.

My Dad, for teaching me the value of working hard, and for giving me the taste for the luxuries in life and a love for travel.

The book was just a dream until Linda Dunscombe came into my life. This lady has so much talent and creativity to bring this all together in record time - of course!

Claire Jenkins, for becoming my right-hand woman in many ways. For her wonderful creative talents. For illustrating the pictures and the front cover and for helping to increase my social presence.

My sister, Samantha Fawdry-Jeffries, and my brother, Nick Palmer, for finally making it a truly family business. I'm prouder of you both than words can ever say.

Rachael and Becky Towers, my first recruits who took 8 years to get started and taught me patience and to never give up on anyone - to travel the world with my best friends will be a privilege.

Barry the Book for encouraging me from day one when I called him with what i thought might be a crazy idea and for helping me to pull it all together.

Andy Waring, Tom Schreiter, and Jayne Leach, for taking the time to read and advise me - your experience is truly appreciated.

My wonderful friend Emma Chatterley who I took on as my PA twelve months ago. You took the pressure off and allowed me to take more time out - thank you for helping everything run smoothly.

And to my contributors, Bob Parker, who is a font of knowledge in the industry. Gemma Easdon and Beth Turner, my dynamic duo where friendship and trust were immediate. Beth Mansfield and Laila Ali for sharing skills I have yet to learn, Claire Spencer for being crazy enough to use Facebook in the first place, just to avoid making a call! And my old school friend, Chris Munro, and his wife Tracey for embracing all that we have developed and being the first to truly run and fly faster than most and are now my wonderful friends.

There would be no Network or no book without the incredible people in my team - thank you for the privilege of being part of my journey and I'm truly humbled by your successes, seeing you fly to greater heights than me will be the icing on the cake.

Special thanks to my first leadership team, Tina Gillies, Faye Daly, Claire Spencer, Debbie Nwangwa and Julianna Woods - there is no 'I' in team - Thank you for your work ethics and your friendships and for keeping me going when times have hurt over the years.

Finally to Will and Rosie - I love you to the moon and back xxxx

Lightning Source UK Ltd.
Milton Keynes UK
UKOW07f0638150115

244507UK00001B/1/P